What People Are Saying About *PlanetHood*

"... read this book. It tells why the ... the planet Earth and how each ... about it."

Robert Stuart
Chairman Emeritus, National Can Company
Chicago, Illinois

"An exceptionally well-written and persuasive book that promotes one of the most rational of human goals—the achievement of planethood in our time. Before we have no time left!"

Albert Ellis, Ph.D.
President, Institute for Rational-Emotive Therapy
Author, *A New Guide to Rational Living*

"*PlanetHood*, by Benjamin B. Ferencz with Ken Keyes, Jr., should be required reading for all of us citizens of the earth. In this remarkable and highly readable book the authors provide a rationale and program of action for meeting the greatest challenge of our time: the choice between nuclear war and planetary suicide, or worldwide peace and growing prosperity."

Garrett R. Carpenter
Professor of Philosophy
Front Range Community College

"The carnage and costs of war and the devastation of the environment this century should convince anyone of the need for a new formula for global security. *PlanetHood* opens the door to give humanity a long-term future on the planet."

Jack Kidd, Major General, USAF (Ret.)
Lecturer and Author
The Strategic Cooperation Initiative

"Governments will not disarm fully until there is an alternative to war. *PlanetHood* explains the peaceful settlement of international disputes. Global environmental disasters cannot be solved on a national basis. There has to be common action on common problems. *PlanetHood* is the route to an environmentally secure future."

Keith D. Suter, Ph.D.
Trinity Peace Research Institute
Perth, Australia

"Prior to reading *PlanetHood*, I felt there was a decent chance we could muddle through without a world government, and that to establish such a government was beyond our powers. My beliefs have been changed. *PlanetHood* is such an important book that I wish I could have written it (though I couldn't have—for I didn't have nearly enough perceptiveness or knowledge)."

Samuel Olanoff, Ph.D.
Professor Emeritus, Physics
Springfield College in Illinois

"*PlanetHood* by Benjamin B. Ferencz and Ken Keyes, Jr. represents a stunning and extremely readable call to action to save not only individual lives but our planet. It is simple, yet profound, and presents a clear-cut program to meet the greatest challenges facing humanity—the very survival of our planet. I think that it is great reading. But far more than that, it is important reading. Those of us who love this planet owe it to ourselves and our children to read this book and then pass it on."

Igor Sikorsky
Attorney at Law
Rocky Hill, Connecticut

"A Celebration of common sense and a joy to read."

Dietrich Fischer
Author, *Preventing War in the Nuclear Age*
Assoc. Professor of Computer Science, Pace University

"This thoughtful, realistic, 'Do-it-yourself' book admirably charts the steps that world leaders and lay citizens must take if humankind is to escape major destruction from modern-age weaponry and ecological irresponsibility. A must for anyone interested in a *legal* rather than a *lethal* world order."

Dr. Burns H. Weston
Professor of Law, University of Iowa
Author, *International Law and World Order*

"*PlanetHood* has furnished us with . . . vital steps that every responsible person should take seriously to preserve our beautiful Mother Earth before it is too late!"

Charles Mercieca, Ph.D.
International Assn. of Educators for World Peace
Author, *Mismanagement in Higher Education*

"PlanetHood is a powerful idea, whose time has come to transform people to enter the 21st century. It is a treasure of valuable ideas from outstanding leaders of the world."

Henry Thiagaraj
Founder, One World Educational Trust
Madras, India

"This is one of the most important books for humanity's future. As a beacon of hope, it offers the keys to our survival and prosperity. Step by practical step, it outlines the cornerstones for a New 21st Century World."

Marc Joyous
Author, *Spaceship Earth: A Crewmember's Guide*
Colorado Springs, Colorado

"In a world that searches for an exit from the seemingly endless conflict in which it wallows, *PlanetHood* offers a vision which can encourage the discouraged."

John N. Hazard, Ph.D.
Professor of Law
Columbia University

"While so many books in this field are just clones of one another, Ferencz and Keyes' creation is unique. It explains the big picture in a most readable way."

Peter Sørensen
Editor, *2000 Millennium Magazine*
Santa Monica, California

"Everyone wants lasting peace; this book tells us what we can *do* to get it."

Anthony D'Amato
Professor of Law
Northwestern University

"Selfhood, neighborhood, nationhood . . . planethood. This book has a compelling and urgent message: the way to save our endangered world from war and suffering is for each of us as members of a world community to become participants, spiritually and politically, in creating its government. *PlanetHood* tells us, compellingly, how we can begin to do our part in this great cause."

Dieter Heinrich
Past President, World Federalists of Canada
Toronto, Canada

PlanetHood
The Key to Your Future

Benjamin B. Ferencz
Ken Keyes, Jr.

Trade Edition

Love Line Books
700 Commercial Avenue
Coos Bay, OR 97420

PlanetHood
is not copyrighted.

Because our lives and all that we hold near and dear can be snuffed out by war or environmental destruction, neither the author nor the publisher will make even one cent from this book. Any surplus above costs will be used to give away copies. We have rearranged our priorities to do our part in preventing the end of the great human adventure of life on this planet.

You are urged to buy copies and give them to your friends. Freely reproduce this book and use it in every way possible. It is our hope that translations in other languages will be made so that all people on earth can hear the good news: **a proven, workable way has been found that will both stop the senseless killing from recurrent wars and effectively avoid environmental ruin.**

1991 Trade Paperback Edition
Printed on long-lasting acid-free paper

Library of Congress Cataloging-in-Publication Data

Ferencz, Benjamin B., 1920-
    PlanetHood : the key to your future / Benjamin B. Ferencz,
Ken Keyes, Jr. -- Rev. 2nd ed.
    p. cm.
    Includes bibliographical references and index.
    ISBN 0-915972-21-2 : $7.95. -- ISBN 0-915972-14-X : $2.50
    1. International organization. 2. Peace. 3. Nuclear dis-
armament. 4. United Nations. I. Keyes, Ken. II. Title.
JX1954.F47 1991   90-13519
327.1'7--dc20   CIP

Love Line Books
700 Commercial Avenue
Coos Bay, OR 97420

To the oppressed
of many lands
who had the courage
to stand up for human freedom
and to those who strive for
a more compassionate world
where peace, dignity, and
a healthy environment
will be the birthright
of all the inhabitants
of this small planet.

CONTENTS

Preface

Ken Keyes, Jr.

The authors don't like prefaces, forewords, or introductions any more than you do. But we ask you not to skip the ones in PlanetHood. Each offers information you need to help create world peace, prosperity, and a livable environment.

Last year, my wife Penny and I were in Costa Rica attending a conference "Seeking the True Meaning of Peace." Among the keynote speakers were Oscar Arias, Nobel Peace Prize winner and then President of Costa Rica, and the Dalai Lama. While there we visited a friend, Carlos Grenados, and his wife Mayra. Carlos is a young medical doctor. He told us he was proud to be a citizen of a country that did not have even one general, admiral, soldier, or marine on its payroll!

> *Never doubt that a small group of thoughtful, committed citizens can change the world. Indeed, it's the only thing that ever has.*
> Margaret Mead

He showed us an old fort in San Jose, the capital, which had been left with bullet holes still in the walls after the civil war of 1948. It is being kept as a wartime ruin to serve as a monument for peace.

Although at that time it had Noriega, a Panamanian dictator, on its southern border, and Ortega, a Nicaraguan dictator, on its northern border, Costa Rica lived in harmony with both its neighbors. I was amazed. Here was a modern nation that had a zero military budget, and yet it had lived in peace with its volatile Central American neighbors for the last forty years. How could this be?

In 1948, a civil war cost some 2,000 lives—the bloodiest event in Costa Rican history. The winning side of this civil war was headed by José Figueres Ferrer and his Social Democratic Party. Without forewarning, in a speech on December 6, 1948 he announced that the army was *no longer needed and would be disbanded!* "It is time," he said, "for Costa Rica to return to her traditional position of having more teachers than soldiers."

He took personal command of the Army and supervised its termination. Figueres said he was abolishing the military "to reaffirm the principle of civil government." They drafted a Constitution guaranteeing free elections with universal suffrage. Article 12 states, "The Army as a permanent institution is proscribed. For vigilance and the preservation of public order, there will be the necessary police forces. Only through *continental agreement* (italics added) for the national defense, may military forces be organized. . . ." Thus on November 7, 1949, by the law of the land, Costa Rica got rid of militarism.

> *Every gun that is made, every warship launched, every rocket fired, signifies in a final sense a theft from those who hunger and are not fed—those who are cold and not clothed. This world in arms is not spending money alone—it is spending the sweat of its laborers, the genius of its scientists, the hopes of its children.*
> Dwight D. Eisenhower, 1953
> Former U.S. President

Figueres became a national hero, winning the first election under the new Constitution. Costa Rica has relied on the *regional guarantees* of the Organization of American States and the Rio Treaty in case another nation violates its borders. It has enjoyed a peace and prosperity that is outstanding in Latin America since it got rid of its military. Indeed, it's a model for the 21st Century for all of us.

The money that would have been used to support the military and buy killing machines has been used instead to provide the people of Costa Rica with one of the Third World's highest levels of education and medical care. In Third World countries, every day a total of 40,000 children under five die of preventable diseases. Yet Costa Ricans have a life expectancy of 67.5 years for men and 71.9 years for women! Its educational system has given its citizens a literacy rate of 93.1%—higher than the literacy rate in the U.S.!

The Hundredth Monkey

In 1982 I wrote a book entitled *The Hundredth Monkey*. Its purpose was to awaken us to the nuclear threat to the future of humanity. There are now over one million copies in print worldwide; it has been published in Norwegian, Dutch, Swedish, Russian, German, Danish, Japanese, Spanish, and Esperanto. We all agree that today's killing technology threatens the survival of humanity through nuclear missiles and poison gas—with possibly even greater horrors yet to be developed—such as murderous laser beams from outer space! To pay for these killing machines, we're ignoring the basic needs of our people and "bankrupting" our nation. And we're destroying our planetary home. So what do we do about it?

> *The military burden makes a dramatic difference in less than a generation. If our policies are not altered, our children will grow up in a second class society, second to Europe and Japan, the military abstainers. Our economy will grow only 35%, while Europe grows 108% and Japan grows 217%."*
>
> Robert W. Reuschlein
> Author, *Peace Economics: Newest Scientific Proof That Military Spending Causes Decline*

PlanetHood is the sequel to *The Hundredth Monkey*. *PlanetHood* describes the only way we have found that can be depended on to give our families a long-term future on Planet Earth. It is not a utopian idea raising false hopes or an untried scheme that depends on enough people suddenly being motivated by friendliness and goodwill—or by fear and panic. It is based on the realistic ways pioneered by the Founding Fathers of the United States in settling disputes *legally* rather than *lethally*.

> The United States should capitalize on the new enlightenment at work in the world by dedicating itself to taking the lead in bringing into being an effective world security arrangement, a world governed by law. The United Nations provides an existing basic structure, but one which requires substantial revamping. To become truly effective, it must be made appropriately representational and vetoless, of course.
>
> Major General Jack Kidd
> United States Air Force, (Ret.)
> Author, *The Strategic Cooperation Initiative*

You will learn that in 1787 the thirteen sovereign colonies in America were in the same predicament as the armed nations of today's world. And you will discover how the political geniuses at the Constitutional Convention in Philadelphia in 1787 solved the problem of how to create *federal unity*—and still have a *precious diversity* in each state. Experts agree that their solution works both nationally and internationally.

These basic techniques have successfully stood the test of time. They've been used *nationally* by the U.S. for over 200 years. Humanity may not survive the 21st Century unless we rapidly apply them *internationally*.

Our present world anarchy must be eliminated.* A world constitution with checks and balances can give us the safest form of governance yet devised to prevent the abuse of power—and to protect our planet. To rescue humanity from war, want, and environmental

* Webster's New Collegiate Dictionary defines anarchy as "absence of government; a state of lawlessness or political disorder due to the absence of governmental authority."

ruin, we must rapidly REPLACE INTERNATIONAL ANARCHY with an international legislature to make laws for global survival, accompanied by international courts and international enforcement.

PlanetHood offers a *practical plan*. This breakthrough book explains eight effective steps you can begin taking immediately to bring a new dimension of abundance and safety into your life and the lives of your family. These steps will help you play your part in a *grassroots movement* that is now gaining momentum. We, the people of the

> *Let us look forward with confidence to the future that is opening before us—a future that, only a short time ago, seemed inconceivable.*
>
> Pérez de Cuéllar, 1990
> U.N. Secretary-General

world, will free ourselves from spending $1.5 million a minute on killing machines! We don't have to be slaves to our savage past.

Our 21st Century

Worldwide excitement is now beginning to build as the year 2000 approaches. This third millennium beckons us to go beyond the killing and callousness of our bloody past. The United Nations has declared 1990 to 1999 "The U.N. Decade of International Law." The possibilities are immense and can hardly be overstated. "Our New Millennium's Resolution," declare Peter Sørensen and Gregory Wright, "must be to insure peace, end suffering, heal the land/sea/air, and generally make the kind of true human progress that previously was forbidden by our isolation and ignorance. We have the physical capacity to achieve these things—and now we have the perfect occasion to do so."*

* *2000 Millennium Magazine,* Winter 1989–1990

"Impossible!" scream those who administer our current military geopolitics. But so was freedom and democracy for Eastern Europe until 1989. When people know what they want and stand up and demand it, our leaders will follow. *They have power because we, the people, give them our power.*

The opportunities facing us are boundless. The decade of the '90s can set the stage for humanity for the next thousand years—and give us and our children a future on this planet. We can make this decade the turning point for humankind.

> As citizens of the human commonwealth ... we have the right to demand that nations submit to law among themselves, just as they require that citizens submit to law inside nations. We have the right to demand that the United Nations become the source of world law, replacing the irrational, irresponsible, and violent behavior of nations with orderly and workable methods for insuring a creative and just peace.
>
> Norman Cousins, President
> World Federalist Association
> Author, *Anatomy of an Illness*

With our satellite TV, fax, and computer networks, the people of this world can no longer be imprisoned in chains of ignorance. Some form of international, political, and military sanity is within our grasp at last. The planethood initiative can solve our life-threatening problems. When the resources wasted in nation-to-nation conflict and posturing are used instead to improve our lot, *we can transform the world.* We're being held back by our obsolete political habits of thinking. But there is a new wind blowing, and it's pushing us toward a safer world of law and order.

Patterns of the Past

It is heartening to compare what we did in 1980 with what happened in 1990. In 1980 Saddam Hussein hurled Iraqi forces at neighboring Iran. Since we were angry about Iran's past seizure of U.S. hostages, many Americans felt "it couldn't happen to a more deserving nation"! So we let this serious violation of international law pass without effective response.

Even when Saddam Hussein gassed his own Kurdish minority and used poison gas against the Iranians, we didn't do what we should have done. The use of poison gas violates conventions ratified by virtually every nation in the world—including Iraq. In addition to enforcement action by the U.N., we should have called for an international criminal court, like the Nuremberg tribunal, and demanded that he be put on trial for his crimes against peace, crimes against humanity, and war crimes.

> *It is time to stop patronizing the people. It is time to stop treating them as children. Peace people are very good at telling us how dangerous the arms race is. It is dangerous, very, very dangerous. We should continue to stress that. But we should also find the courage to tell people how radical the necessary remedy for the arms race is and why that radical remedy is necessary.*
> Dr. John Logue
> Director, Common Heritage Inst.

Failing to punish criminals encourages more crime. If our President had led the United Nations to oppose Saddam Hussein when he first became an international outlaw, we could have *set a good example for the world by supporting international law.* We could have shown Hussein that international criminals will be opposed by the world community—by force if necessary. *This would probably have prevented the invasion of Kuwait—and saved us from sending our boys to defend Saudi Arabia!*

However, since the U.S. support for international law seemed weak or hypocritical, Hussein got the message that he could run wild—and the international community would remain aloof. This has cost us dearly.

When Iraq again committed aggression by invading Kuwait on August 2, 1990, we were worried about our oil supply. President Bush moved like lightning to demand action by the U.N. Security Council. Within 75 minutes after the meeting began, the Council acted unanimously and ordered Iraq to withdraw immediately. When Iraq failed to respond, the Council unanimously imposed comprehensive economic sanctions, which were accepted by almost the entire international community. What a change! Finally, the U.N. Charter was beginning to be used as we intended—to restore peace.

> Since wars begin in the minds of men, it is in the minds of men that we have to erect the ramparts of peace.
>
> UNESCO Charter

True, we moved our own military forces into position without waiting for Security Council authorization. But President Bush made it clear that we were lawfully responding to a request for protection from Saudi Arabia. Our actions were intended to deter further aggression and to defend the area while we reinforced our endangered allies in the region. The U.S. sought to act only in conjunction with other nations consistent with Security Council resolutions.

The Charter of the U.N. permits it to have an armed peacekeeping force to deter or respond to aggression. However the Security Council to date has not authorized the U.N. to hire a single soldier! Therefore the world still depends on the military of individual nations to act as volunteer vigilantes. Would you feel safe with a police department in your city that had no paid officers, but depended on volunteers to step forth whenever there was a murder?

World Law and Order

When Iraq invaded Kuwait, the world turned to the United Nations as never before. In almost every statement made by President Bush, he referred to the need to uphold international law. The U.N. responded promptly and courageously in an effort to restore peace without the use of military force. This seems like an auspicious beginning to the "U.N. Decade of International Law."

We think President Bush was right in opposing Hussein's aggression. But if he did it only to keep down the price of oil, that was the wrong reason. A more inspiring and important justification would be to establish law and order in the world. Unfortunately, the United States often gives the impression that it is interested in getting rid of tyrants and world anarchy only in cases where our own pocketbook or ideology is threatened. Let us hope that sacrifices made in the Middle East will herald a new dawn where the rule of law will begin to govern all nations.

> Our ideal is a world community of states with political systems and foreign policies based on law.
>
> Mikhail Gorbachev
> Soviet General Secretary
> Address to the U.N.
> December 7, 1988

For our future well-being, we must create a vision of a lawful world. It is noble to oppose aggression—and even use force if lawfully authorized by the United Nations of the world. Under international law, we should respond to all aggression—even when one's own particular interests are not *directly* affected.

How soon will we learn that international crimes must be stopped *anywhere and everywhere* if we are to create a world of law that is safe for our children? The present international anarchy encourages dictators to plunder. No one is secure in an ungoverned world without an international system of law. Our government's frequently blasé attitude toward international criminals fails to protect your family or your pocketbook in our modern interdependent world.

> *The very triumph of scientific annihilation has destroyed the possibility of war being a medium of practical settlement of international differences . . . . If you lose, you are annihilated. If you win, you stand only to lose. War contains the germs of double suicide . . . . Military alliances, balances of power, leagues of nations all in turn have failed . . . . We have our last chance. If we will not devise some greater and more equitable system, Armageddon will be at our door.*
>
> Douglas MacArthur
> General, U.S. Army

So we cannot yet depend upon the politicians to help us toward planethood. They are usually dedicated to protecting their separate partisan, parochial, or local interests as they perceive them. Their thinking habits tend toward the old style of defense: if you want peace, prepare for war. They usually rely on the old jungle law of might makes right. They think in terms of *lethal* instead of *legal* ways to settle disputes between nations.

What Won't Work

To reach our full human destiny, we must clear away the mental cobwebs of the past in which we are ensnared. We must understand, as Emery Reves pointed out, that world peace and national security cannot be achieved through armament—*or even disarmament!* In spite of Costa Rica's noble example, how can our President, who is responsible for the security of the

U.S., trust all the other 159 nations enough to completely disarm?

After the tragedy of World War I, the most powerful nations on earth discussed disarmament treaties, which led to the Great Disarmament Conference of 1932 in Geneva. The United States, Britain, and France in the pursuit of peace cut down substantially on their military firepower.

> The world no longer has a choice between force and law. If civilization is to survive, it must choose the rule of law.
> Dwight D. Eisenhower
> Former U.S. President

However, it only takes one fanatic like a Hitler (or Qaddafi, Saddam Hussein, or Pol Pot) with today's killing technology to start an arms race or war leading to mass extermination.

When a nation relies on guns and other killing machines for "defense," history shows that its politicians will eventually use them to settle disputes, intimidate, or conquer more territory. Generals and politicians have a notorious track record for overestimating their own strength to kill and conquer—and underestimating the strength of their targets. Think of Hitler in World War II, the Japanese at Pearl Harbor, the Argentinians in the Falklands, and Saddam Hussein in Iran.

Our politicians have tried to create peace through a "balance of power." They've used a theory of deterrence (Mutual Assured Destruction, otherwise known as MAD). *But one country's deterrence is another country's incentive to start an arms race!* And our planet's still stuck with a war system—piously sold to the public in the name of "defense."

The nuclear bomb has been given credit for preventing an all-out catastrophic war since the end of World War II. This may be an illusion; conventional arms also produced an armed stalemate for 44 years between 1870 (the Franco-Prussian War) and 1914 (when World War I began).

What Will Work

So the human race has tried everything except the one thing that will work to keep the peace and preserve the ecology: *to replace international "Wild West" anarchy with international law.* As you examine the eight exciting steps that *you can take* to give us a good future, you may be amazed at how near we are to our goal—

> We must create world-wide law and law enforcement as we outlaw world-wide war and weapons.
>
> John F. Kennedy, U.S. President

and how much your voice is needed at this crucial period of humanity's growth.

More and more people are realizing that if we really want world peace, plenty, and planethood, we must have an international congress to make laws, international courts to administer justice, and international enforcement to apprehend the lawbreakers.

While so many have been pessimistic about the wanton destruction of human life and the environment, we are inspired by the exciting vision of planethood through enforceable world law. As you'll discover in Step Four, the foundation of world law has been created by the work of many pioneers during the past two centuries. It's there waiting for us to begin using it.

Grassroots understanding and support is urgently needed to erect the structure of planethood as the 21st Century approaches. Through the Eight Steps, we can make a great difference to the future of humanity. When the Third Millennium dawns a few years from now, we can have the satisfaction of knowing that, like Paul Revere, we have awakened our sleeping neighbors and saved ourselves.

Building National Strength

In the 20th Century, we have been afraid of foreign attack. In the 21st Century, we have more to fear from ruining our environment and charging trillions of dollars for killing machines on our national credit card. In the next century our national

> *Henceforth, every nation's foreign policy must be judged at every point by one consideration: does it lead us to a world of law and order or does it lead us back to anarchy and death?*
>
> Albert Einstein

strength will lie in our economic vitality; citizen education; public health; solving the drug, food, and housing problems; eliminating discrimination; lifting our society from the pits of crime and individual and corporate sleaze; creating social justice; uniting our nation through understanding and cooperation; and becoming a part of a **system of mutual security for all nations.**

This breakthrough book will explain why foresighted U.S. presidents, generals, admirals, and scientists tell us that a system of world law will give us *more security and national defense* than our costly army, navy, air force, and Star Wars combined.

Neighborhood—statehood—nationhood— planethood. ALL ARE NEEDED TO PROTECT US IN TODAY'S WORLD.

This is a do-it-yourself manual. The future of yourself and your family is too important to leave to anyone else. It's time to give up hoping others will do the job for you. You can make your life count as one of the Founding Mothers—or Fathers—of a new world system that ensures permanent peace and plenty on a sustainable Planet Earth.

Foreword

Robert Muller

Robert Muller is a former Assistant Secretary-General of the United Nations, which he served for 38 years. He is a noted author, lecturer, and educator. His books include Most of All They Taught Me Happiness, New Genesis, What War Taught Me About Peace, *and* A World Core Curriculum. *He is also the Chancellor of the University for Peace in San Jose, Costa Rica.*

If a divine or extraterrestrial committee of experts in planetary management visited our Earth, they would not believe their eyes.

"You are insane!" they would exclaim. "This is no way to administer a planet! We give you the lowest mark in planetary management in the entire universe."

We would look at them with surprise, astonished by the vehemence of their attack.

"Look at what you are doing!" they would add with gentleness and pity. "You were given one

> *A world that has become a single geographic unit is now groping its way, however slowly, toward global institutions as the only way of achieving common safety and common progress. A new world is waiting to be born.*
> Norman Cousins, President
> World Federalist Association
> Author, *Anatomy of an Illness*

of the most beautiful planets in the cosmos—one of the rare celestial homes, at the right distance from a sun, endowed with marvelous forms of life. It is a living planet with an atmosphere, fertile soils, waters, and oceans. It is vibrant and interdependent, with elements that are all interlinked in the most marvelous ways. A true jewel in the universe. And look what you have done with it:

1. You have divided this planet into 160 separate territorial fragments without rhyme or reason—without geographic, ecological, human, or any other logic. All these fragments are sovereign; i.e., *each of them considers itself*

more important than the planet and the rest of humanity.

2. You have armed these fragments to their teeth in order to defend their so-called "integrity." They often steal a piece of land from their neighbors.

3. You let two of the biggest parts of this international jigsaw puzzle stuff the surface and the inside of the earth, the waters, the seas, the airs, and tomorrow the heavens and the stars with nuclear devices capable of destroying most of the life on this planet.

4. You permit ego-driven tyrants to snuff out lives with poison gas.

5. You put some of your best minds to work designing more efficient ways to kill—instead of better ways to nurture one's body, mind, and spirit.

6. You spend huge sums of money for each of these sovereign territories, and almost nothing to safeguard and provide for the needs of the planet as a whole. You do not even have a planetary budget! What an aberration!

7. You let many of your scientists, industrialists, developers, builders, promoters, merchants, and military progressively destroy the fundamental resources of your planet, so that within a few decades it will become unlivable—and you will die like flies.

8. You educate your children as if each of these territories were an autonomous island floating on an ocean—instead of teaching them about their planet, which is their home, and about humanity, which is their family.

They would have a long list of other grievances: the gaps between the rich and the poor, between the overfed and the hungry; violence in so many forms; self-destructive drugs; the radioactive and chemical poisoning of the planet; ruthless greed for money and power regardless of the harm to fellow humans and animals; the violation by states of individual human rights; refugees; tortures; abandoned children; the homeless; the absence of a philosophy of life, of ethics, of planetary morals; a youth without ideals; racism; misinformation by the media and governments; abusive monopolies; and an unlimited imagination to dress our own nation or group with every possible virtue and greatness while at the same time denigrating and dividing other nations and groups.

> *We are still a long way from [what Abraham Lincoln called] that 'family of man.' In fact, we seem to be receding from the ideal rather than growing closer to it. Interests of all kinds—personal, selfish, state, nation, group, and, if you like, company interests— still considerably outweigh genuinely common and global interests. We are still under the sway of the destructive and vain belief that man is the pinnacle of creation and not just a part of it and that therefore everything is permitted.*
> Vaclav Havel
> President of Czechoslovakia
> Address to U.S. Congress

We could offer many arguments to explain how we got this way: our checkered history; the current nation-states being the result of conquests, murders, stealings, invasions, wars, and marriages; the recent discovery, only 500 years ago, that we are a globe rotating around its sun rather than the contrary; the dearth of global data until the United Nations and its specialized agencies were born; a total inexperience in planetary management; the absence of any precedents; the novelty of the crises, challenges, and global problems to which we react like little children burning our fingers; a first very weak world organization, misunderstood, used as a scapegoat by its masters, who monopolize all fiscal resources of the planet; belief in obsolete values and ideologies; the multitude of tongues, cultures, beliefs, and religions that we have inherited from the past; and so on.

The extraterrestrials would answer, "All right. You have extenuating circumstances due to your history and slow evolution. But this has lasted long enough. You have until the year 2000—the date of entry into your next millennium. Sit down. Think. Bring together your best minds. Consult your populations. And make a blueprint for a better system of planetary management. Luckily you have many excellent resources available.

> *My humanity is bound up in yours, for we can only be human together.*
> Archbishop Desmond Tutu
> Nobel Peace Prize, 1984

"The latest is *PlanetHood*, a book by Benjamin Ferencz and Ken Keyes. *PlanetHood* seems to us a good point of departure. That book raises in effect the following fundamental question: What would be the fate of the United States if each of its fifty states were sovereign and possessed an army, navy, and air force, a President, a Supreme Court, a State Department, a national hymn, a national flag, national days, and a Congress? What if the United States government were no more than a United Nations without sovereignty; without legislative, executive, judicial, and fiscal powers; unable to make laws or decisions, but only recommendations and exhortations? You would exclaim: 'What an indescribable mess it would be!' Well, this is exactly the state of your planet torn up into 160 pieces!

"We will return in ten years, during your celebration of the Bimillennium. We hope that by the year 2000 you will have drawn up a proper political and administrative regime for this planet.

"Do not lose any time. Be courageous. Do not get stopped by the antiquated beliefs carefully nurtured by the existing powers and all those who benefit from the present disorder.

"You are on the eve of major potential nuclear, ecological, and climatic disasters. May God protect you, bless you, and guide you. After all, you are our brothers and sisters. May cosmic enlightenment finally illuminate your marvelous little planet circling faithfully around its sun in the vast universe.

> *There are no boundaries in the real Planet Earth. No United States, no Soviet Union, no China, no Taiwan, East Germany or West. Rivers flow unimpeded across the swaths of continents. The persistent tides—the pulse of the sea—do not discriminate; they push against all the varied shores on Earth.*
> Captain Jacques-Yves Cousteau
> Oceanographer and Explorer

"And please remember," they would advise as they left, "this planet has not been created for you. You were created to take good care of it."

Introduction

Benjamin B. Ferencz

All humanity has a right to live in peace and dignity—regardless of race, religion, or political persuasion. A sketch of my life shows how I came to this view and why I invite you to help stop the errors of the past, and create a new future for humanity in the 21st Century.

Transylvania to "Hell's Kitchen"

I was born in a small and primitive farmhouse in a remote village of the Carpathian mountains of Transylvania. Few people even know where that is. For most, images of dark forests and bloodthirsty monsters come to mind. Indeed, many legends have been built on this foundation. Before World War I, Transylvania was part of the Austro-Hungarian Empire. For unknown reasons, my father bore the same name as the Emperor—Ferencz Jozsef (Franz Josef). Unfortunately, the similarity began and ended right there. My family was noble only in spirit. When Hungary gave up parts of Transylvania to Romania, my family feared increased persecution of Jewish minorities and decided to seek safety and fortune elsewhere. I was ten months old when, in the cold of January 1921, we set sail for "The Golden Land of Opportunity"—America.

We arrived in New York harbor penniless and were awakened from our dream of plenty to the same harsh reality that faced millions of immigrants. With no knowledge of the language or special skills, life was not easy. My earliest memories recall our small basement apartment in a Manhattan district—appropriately referred to as "Hell's Kitchen." Even in the worst of times, though, there was never any doubt that America was an infinite improvement over any other place we knew.

I spent most of my early years in the New York public school system. Since I was too small to play most sports, I spent much of my free time in the library. I also remember going to the New York Society for Ethical Culture on Sundays to hear sermons that stressed the brotherhood of all people. Even at an early age, I felt a deep yearning for universal friendship and world peace.

> MAKE US EFFECTIVE AND USEFUL FOR THE AD-VANCEMENT OF THE CAUSE OF PEACE AND JUSTICE AND LIBERTY IN THE WORLD.
> Inscription over a portal at the Harvard Law School Library

I was enrolled in a special high school with an accelerated curriculum. My training there qualified me for an academic scholarship to the New York City College. It was a proud day for my family when four years later I acquired a degree in social sciences.

My only ambition during those early years was to become a lawyer. I considered myself fortunate, therefore, to be admitted to Harvard Law School. I managed to win a scholarship and earned my keep by waiting on tables, tutoring, and doing research for one of my professors, a leading criminologist writing a book on war crimes. Through him I acquired an expertise that was to have a profound influence on my later life.

Normandy Beach to Dachau

The United States Army had little use for lawyers when America entered World War II. After I graduated from Harvard in 1943, I joined an antiaircraft artillery battalion preparing for the invasion of France. I was to return to my native continent, though not under the best of circumstances. I plunged into the sea at "Omaha Beach" in Normandy and was baptized by the tide of a world at war. As an enlisted man under General Patton, I fought in every campaign in Europe.

Despite the perils and hardships, I did not fully grasp the horrors of war until we began to uncover evidence of Nazi atrocities. I was soon transferred to a newly created War Crimes Branch of the Army to gather evidence of Nazi brutality and apprehend the criminals. It was only then that my unique knowledge of war crimes law was at last put to use.

It was a grisly assignment. Among my duties, I had to dig up bodies of young American flyers who had parachuted or crashed, and were beaten to death by enraged German mobs or murdered by local Gestapo officials. This, however, was merely the initiation to horrors yet to come. It was not until I joined the American troops advancing toward German concentration camps that I realized the full extent of the Nazi terror.

> *The dream of a world united against the awful wastes of war is . . . deeply imbedded in the hearts of men everywhere.*
> Woodrow Wilson
> Former U.S. President
> When advocating the
> League of Nations

Indelibly seared into my memory are the scenes I witnessed while liberating these centers of death and destruction. Camps like Buchenwald, Mauthausen, and Dachau are vividly imprinted in my mind's eye. Even today, when I close my eyes, I witness a deadly vision I can never forget—the crematoria aglow with the fire of burning flesh, the mounds of emaciated corpses stacked like cordwood waiting to be burned. *Most of all, though, I will never forget the stench of rotting and burning bodies.*

It was often impossible to tell whether the skeleton-like inmates lying near-naked in the dust were dead or alive. Those who could walk had been whisked away by panic-stricken SS guards. Their flight was made visible only by the trail of dead bodies strewn along the road. The bedraggled prisoners who could not keep pace with the retreat were shot on the spot and left dead or dying. I helped to uncover many mass graves where innocent victims had been massacred.

> *Let us be . . . cherishing our cultural and folkloric diversity, but not letting these differences become the source and instruments of hatred, divisions and wars.*
>
> Robert Muller
> Former U.N. Asst. Sec.-Gen.

I had peered into Hell. *I had seen the brutalizing effects of man's inhumanity to man.* As I went about my grim duties, I was filled with a silent numbness. It was as if my mind had built an emotional wall to avoid going mad. There were no tears or wild cries for vengeance. *But the days of my laughing boyhood were over.*

History's Biggest Murder Trial

On the day after Christmas 1945, I was honorably discharged from the U.S. Army with the rank of Sergeant of Infantry. I returned to New York and prepared to practice law. Shortly thereafter, I received a telegram inviting me to come to the Pentagon in Washington. There I met Colonel "Mickey" Marcus, a flamboyant West Pointer who had been a District Attorney in New York. He was recruiting lawyers for the Nuremberg war crimes trials.

The trial against Goering and other Nazi leaders was already in progress. He urged me to go back to Germany as a civilian prosecutor for the United States, offering me the simulated rank of Colonel. I joined the staff of Colonel (later General) Telford Taylor, a Harvard Law man with a distinguished legal background. The U.S. had decided to prosecute a broad cross section of Nazi criminals once the trial against Goering and his henchmen was over. Taylor was to be the Chief of Counsel for a dozen subsequent Nuremberg trials, which had to be prepared in a hurry.

Taylor sent me with about fifty researchers to Berlin to scour Nazi offices and archives. No one could be indicted without evidence of personal guilt beyond any reasonable doubt. The records we uncovered were to form the basis for trials against German doctors, lawyers, judges, generals, industrialists, and others who played leading roles in organizing or perpetrating Nazi brutalities.

One day, one of our investigators was stunned by the discovery of a number of files uncovered in the cellar of the burned-out Gestapo headquarters. They were top secret reports chronicling the number of people slaughtered by special SS extermination squads called *Einsatzgruppen*. Their crimes were horrendous. Without pity or remorse, the SS murder squads killed every Jewish man, woman, and child they could lay their hands on. Gypsies, communist functionaries, and Soviet intellectuals suffered the same fate. *I tabulated over a million persons*

> *I know war as few other men now living know it, and nothing to me is more revolting. I have long advocated its complete abolition as its very destructiveness on both friend and foe has rendered it useless as a means of settling international disputes.*
> General Douglas MacArthur
> Address to U.S. Congress
> upon retiring after 52 years

deliberately murdered by these special "action groups." The disclosure of unmitigated cruelty screamed out for justice. I flew to Nuremberg with the evidence and presented it to General Taylor, who bore the final responsibility for the prosecutions.

In our hands lay overwhelming evidence of Nazi genocide. The General immediately recognized the vast importance and impact these documents would have. We vowed not to allow these mass murderers to escape trial. The case was assigned to me. I became Chief Prosecutor for the United States in what the Associated Press called "the biggest murder trial in history." Twenty-two defendants were charged with murdering over a million people. I was only twenty-seven years old. It was my first case.

> *The defendants in the dock were the cruel executioners, whose terror wrote the blackest page in human history. Death was their tool and life was their toy. If these men be immune, then law has lost its meaning and man must live in fear.*
>
> Benjamin B. Ferencz
> Opening Statement
> Einsatzgruppen Trial
> Nuremberg, 1947

What sentence could I possibly ask the court to impose for such crimes? How does one draw a balance between the lives of twenty-two guilty Germans and their horrendous crimes against humanity? It seemed that hanging the lot was not enough. The significance of these proceedings should have an impact on the future. The entire human race had to be protected from the lawlessness of tyrants.

"May it please Your Honors," I said as I addressed the tribunal, "it is with sorrow and with hope that we here disclose the deliberate slaughter of more than a million innocent and defenseless men, women, and children. This was the tragic fulfillment of a program of intolerance and arrogance. Vengeance is not our goal, nor do we seek merely a just retribution. *We ask this Court to affirm by international penal action man's right to live in peace and dignity regardless of his race or creed. The case we present is a plea of humanity to law.*"

The trial lasted a year and a half; all of the defendants were convicted. Thirteen were sentenced to death. The verdict was hailed as a great success for the prosecution. My primary objective had been to establish *a legal precedent that would encourage a more humane and secure world in the future.*

Though many of the Nazi atrocities were carried out by nothing less than sadists or professional criminals, those who conceived and directed the extermination programs were quite different. I was shocked to learn that almost all of them were educated men who seemed quite normal. They loved their families, were kind to cats and dogs, enjoyed Wagner's music, and could quote Goethe's poetry. In fact, many of them—I am ashamed to say—were lawyers.

Even today, as I look back upon this dark chapter in human history, I am dumbfounded by the complete lack of remorse with which these white-collar mass murderers seemed to operate. Regret was practically nonexistent, while denial of the truth, self-pity, and false accusations against others were commonplace. I soon realized that if one begins with the distorted conviction that a person of a certain race, opinion, or belief is inferior, his extermination seems logical and even desirable.

Nuremberg taught me that creating a world of tolerance and compassion would be a long and arduous task. And I also learned that if we did not devote ourselves to developing effective world law, the same cruel mentality that made the Holocaust possible might one day destroy the entire human race.

The Pen Versus the Sword

In 1970, with the United States sinking ever deeper into the quagmire of Vietnam, it was only natural that my mind should turn to the *need for a peaceful world.* Over fifty thousand young Americans died there for reasons that a significant segment of the American population didn't support. Combatants on both sides accused each other (as they do in all wars) of aggression and crimes against humanity. After careful deliberation, I decided that I would gradually withdraw from the private practice of law and would dedicate myself to studying and writing about world peace.

> *We appeal as human beings to human beings: Remember your humanity, and forget the rest.*
> Albert Einstein
> Last public statement, 1955

True loyalty does not demand blind obedience. "My country right or wrong" is a prescription for national decay. As the Germans under Hitler learned, it could be a recipe for disaster. Citizenship and true patriotism carry a duty to encourage your country when it is right and *to help it when it has gone astray.* I was determined to try to make my adopted country more responsive to the needs and aspirations of all its citizens so that it could remain a continuing inspiration to the peoples of the world.

Books for Peace

My book *Defining International Aggression—The Search for World Peace* was published in 1975. It seemed to me that there was little sense in denouncing aggression, terrorism, and other crimes against humanity unless these offenses became part of an accepted international criminal code enforced by an international court. I wrote another two-volume documentary history, *An International Criminal Court—A Step Toward World Peace*, which was published in 1980. It was intended to be a tool that nations could use to build a structure for peace.

While still at Harvard, I had studied jurisprudence with Professor Roscoe Pound, one of the most

> *However intense may be a group's moral conviction of the rightness of its particular religion or ideology, it should in its own interest function within the universally accepted system of law and politics aimed at order and justice.*
>
> Quincy Wright, 1962
> Professor of International Law
> University of Chicago

learned jurists in the world. In the back of my mind, his wise teaching remained. He believed that *no regime could be considered lawful unless it contained three components: codes, courts, and enforcement.* To complete the trilogy, I needed to study the problem of enforcement. So back I went to the libraries and U.N. meetings.

Three floors beneath the U.N. building in New York are the archives of the League of Nations. Here there are thousands of old books dealing with war and peace. I obtained a key to the rooms in which these treasures were kept. For long days and nights I sat there alone probing the wisdom of many scholars *who had devoted their minds to the greatest problem that still vexed humankind.* The results of my research were recorded in another two-volume book, *Enforcing International Law—A Way to World Peace*, which was published in 1983.

My books were intended primarily for university libraries, government officials, professors of law or political science, and policymakers of all nations. The six volumes contain the details and documents to show that a world of international law, courts, and effective enforcement is both necessary and feasible as we move into the 21st Century. In order to spread the word to a larger audience, I condensed the gist of my thinking into a small, inexpensive paperback, *A Common Sense Guide to World Peace*. The title was influenced by that great patriot, Tom Paine, whose pamphlet *Common Sense* had inspired the American Revolution. On October 25, 1985, I sent the first copies to President Reagan and General Secretary Gorbachev of the Soviet Union. Like Tom Paine, *I hoped my writing would serve the interests of humanity.* •

> *The central task of our time is to evolve a new system of world order based on principles of peace and justice.*
>
> Richard Falk, 1983
> Professor of Law
> Princeton University

Where We Stand Today

As we enter the last decade of this century, the world faces a great social transformation. Dramatic strides toward planethood have been made in the past few years. They reflect the rising power of the individual asserting fundamental rights.

Eastern Europe has cast off the yoke of tyranny. Outraged citizens have torn down the Berlin wall. Europe is racing toward economic and parliamentary integration. People everywhere yearn for freedom and prosperity. President Bush and General Secretary Gorbachev, facing enormous economic burdens, have agreed to reverse the arms race. Confrontation between the two superpowers has ended. Britain's Prime Minister, Margaret Thatcher, has declared the Cold

War over. The speed of these changes was inconceivable only a few years ago.

To be sure, wars will continue to disgrace the human landscape. Unfortunately, deep-rooted habits of aggression and inhumanity are not easily erased. The forces of nationalism, militarism, ethnic hatred, intolerance, and arrogance will continue to take their traditional toll in the blood of innocents. Our call for a more humane society ruled by law, courts, and effective enforcement is not yet a reality. Until that day comes, helpless victims will continue to pay the price in misery and suffering. Yet, throughout the

> *The events of the year just ended, the Revolution of '89, have begun a chain reaction, changes so striking that it marks the beginning of a new era in the world's affairs.*
>
> President George Bush
> State of the Union Message
> January 31, 1990

world there is a visible and growing awareness that as we approach the next century, the force of law *must* replace the law of force or we shall all perish.

On August 2, 1990, Iraq (which had gotten away with the 1980 invasion of Iran and the illegal use of poison gas in 1988) invaded its peaceful Arab neighbor Kuwait. Within 11 hours—at 4:45 in the morning—the Security Council of the United Nations was convened. Within 75 minutes, by unanimous vote, the invasion was condemned and Iraq was ordered to withdraw all of its forces "immediately and unconditionally." Never before had the Council acted with such speed and clarity.

Four days later, when Iraq failed to comply, the Council unanimously ordered all states to impose strict economic sanctions against Iraq and not to recognize any puppet regime they might set up. If that didn't work, further steps would be considered within thirty days.

Nation-states all around the world, including most Arab states, agreed to comply with the boycott. The United States and other nations immediately moved troops and ships into defensive positions around Iraq. The distrust that previously had blocked effective action by the Council was gone. The Council

> *The great challenge of the '90s ... is to salvage and improve the U.N. and to develop it into an agency capable of providing effective justice among nations—an agency, moreover, capable of meeting the wide range of serious problems that are inherent in a world that has become a single geographic unit.*
> Norman Cousins, President
> World Federalist Association
> Author, *Anatomy of an Illness*

was finally able to activate collective security measures in the manner intended when the U.N. Charter was adopted in 1945. What a change!

Additional resolutions, reached *unanimously* by the Security Council, slowly began to draw a tighter noose around Iraq. On August 27, 1990, the Soviet Union, which had been one of the arms suppliers to Iraq, described the successful functioning of the U.N. system as "a historical and unprecedented phenomenon in modern politics, [providing] a unique opportunity for the creation of effective mechanisms to uphold law and justice in international relations."

There will undoubtedly be difficult times ahead. But there is growing recognition of the importance of the United Nations in helping to maintain peace—and to manage this planet in a rational way. U.N. Secretary-General de Cuéllar—whose office has been flooded with PlanetHood Proclamations (See Appendix 4)—described it in his 1989 Report as "the birth of a new kind of loyalty, an Earth-Patriotism, a looking at the planet and its atmosphere as an object for protection and not for aggression and pillage."

It will take time, determination, and effort, but with your help, a peaceful and prosperous world governed by international law can be achieved.

Planethood is on the march!

1st Step

Insist on
Your Ultimate
Human Right

The ancient Greeks had a legend about a nice guy named Damocles, who sat down to enjoy a great feast. The table was loaded with all known delicacies. Everything was perfect—except for one thing. Suspended above his head was a sharp-pointed sword held by only a single hair! THIS IS YOU AND ME TODAY!

We live in a world in which many people enjoy comfortable living conditions that even a monarch of old could not duplicate—TV, air conditioning, automobiles, health care, etc. Yet we greatly limit our prosperity and threaten our future with the way we run the planet today. *We globally waste $1.5 million every minute* on mass killing machines. We are raping our natural resources, ruining the ozone layer, and ravishing the ecosystem.

We stand on the threshold of an enormous increase of good things beyond the levels of the past or present: potentially more

> *Our world is prodigiously healthy and vigorous, and terribly sick at the same time. The extraordinary upsurge and economic expansion of the past fifteen years . . . give hope of unprecedented progress and welfare. The malady that may destroy everybody, and everything is caused exclusively by our totally outdated political institutions—in flagrant contradiction to the economic and technological realities of our time.*
> Emery Reves
> The Anatomy of Peace

freedom, security, education, material comfort, and entertainment, to mention only a few. Yet the future of humanity has never been so threatened.

1

In the U.S. we are inundated with individual rights: women's rights, men's rights, children's rights, workers' rights, employers' rights—even the spotted owl has rights! But with all these rights, something is profoundly wrong. *We don't have the basic right to live with dignity in a healthy environment free from the threat of war!*

There is not even one court on the planet that protects this ultimate human right. Unless this paradox is rapidly corrected, humanity may not be around much longer.

PlanetHood is your personal how-to-do-it instruction book. It spells out how you can give yourself and your family a life of lasting peace and *unparalleled personal prosperity.* This book explains the Eight Steps you can begin taking immediately to create a world with a wonderful future. It presents a positive and practical way to replace the present system of stabbing and grabbing with a planethood system of caring and sharing.

> *Why are we raising so insistently the question of a universal system of international peace and security? Because we cannot reconcile ourselves to the situation in which the world finds itself on the threshold of the third millennium—threatened with destruction, in a state of constant tension, an atmosphere of suspicion and discord, expending the enormous resources, labour and talent of millions of people in order to increase mutual mistrust and fear. People can talk as much as they like about the need for halting the arms race, and eliminating militarism, and about cooperation, but nothing will change unless we start to act.*
>
> Mikhail Gorbachev
> Soviet General Secretary
> U.N. Address, September 1987

Two Great Perils We Face

There are two ways in which humanity can be wiped off this planet—the fast way and the slow way:

2

The fast way is through nuclear war, which not only kills millions of innocent people but also brings on nuclear winter, destroys the ozone layer, poisons the air, vaporizes anything nearby, sets off uncontrollable fire storms, and has other aftereffects both known and unknown.

The slow way is through the deterioration of our oceans, lands, and atmosphere by our present ignorant and heedless destruction of the environment. Continued trashing of the planet can result in an uninhabitable world for our children.

In spite of all the gloom and doom, *PlanetHood* offers you a practical, life-enriching solution. This book will describe the steps we must take to forever remove "the scourge of war" from this earth! And we will find that the same solution that rescues us from the devastation of international war will also enable us to solve our environmental problems.

It is great news to find a single solution that will enable us to solve both of humanity's most pressing problems!

So let's take a look at our current predicament. Then we'll describe how you can empower yourself to help rescue humanity from the cosmic wastebasket.

The Present International Anarchy

As we've pointed out, we live today in a world of international anarchy. Most nations are loading up with all the killing machines they can afford—*or can't afford.* Five nations now acknowledge having nuclear weapons (U.S., Soviet Union, England, France, China), and 52 nations have nuclear research facilities that in the 21st Century can enable them to join the nuclear club.

What will our world be like in a few years if the Hitlers, Saddam Husseins, and Pol Pots get these devastating weapons? According to Charles Ebinger of Georgetown University's Center for Strategic and International Studies, "It's probably the most pessimistic issue I've ever dealt with. Nobody seems to come up with any solutions, myself included."

The U.S. military has developed a 58-pound nuclear "backpack" bomb

> With all my heart I believe that the world's present system of sovereign nations can lead only to barbarism, war and inhumanity.
>
> Albert Einstein

that can be carried by one person. The principles for building nuclear bombs are known throughout the world. Do you want your children to live in a world in which only one "terrorist" or "freedom fighter" can kill more people in an hour than a whole army used to kill in a year?

Every year the people of the world are taxed to spend about $1,000,000,000,000 for military purposes. There are over 50,000 nuclear devices on earth with an explosive capacity of 15,000 to 20,000 million tons of TNT. Since the world population is just over 5 billion, that works out to an average of 3 to 4 TONS of TNT waiting to kill each man, woman, and child on earth!

Disarmament Alone Won't Work

Disarmament only affects some of the *symptoms* of the cancer of war: the killing machinery. It does not in any way get rid of the cancer itself: settling disagreements by war. This cancer will eventually kill us if we don't do something about it. We must not be

AMERICA'S DOOMSDAY MACHINE

Just one of the 192 nuclear warheads aboard the U.S. missile submarine Tennessee, currently at sea, would be enough to flatten the Kremlin and every building within half a mile if detonated 6,000 ft. over Moscow. Up to two miles from ground zero, all but the toughest structures would be destroyed, and even as far as four miles away, wood and brick buildings would collapse and burst into flames. But that devastation is not sufficient for the Pentagon. U.S. nuclear-attack plans call for raining 120 warheads on Moscow alone—a level of targeting, says veteran arms expert Peter Zimmerman, that "isn't strategy, it's pathology."

The more than 15,000 sites targeted in the Soviet Union are outlined in what Arkansas Democratic Senator Dale Bumpers last week called the "most closely guarded secret in America"—the Single Integrated Operational Plan. The so-called SIOP, or "doomsday book," designates facilities in the Soviet Union that are to be incinerated and the kinds of U.S. missiles and planes that will carry out each attack. It divides Soviet targets into four categories: nuclear forces; other military targets; 105,000 ranking members of the Soviet military, political and managerial élite; and war-supporting industries such as factories and depots.

After hearing figures like this, a reflective President John Kennedy muttered, "And we call ourselves the human race."

From *Time*, July 16, 1990

5

hypnotized into a false confidence that disarmament alone solves the problem of war.

Let's suppose all nuclear weapons were removed from the face of the earth through 100% nuclear disarmament by all the 160 nations of this world. *Humanity would still be in trouble.* The killing technology of today, even with nonnuclear weapons, is *far more deadly* than anything used during World War II until Hiroshima and Nagasaki. Chemical warfare (poison gas) and biological warfare (deadly germs and viruses) can rival nuclear killing potential. How long will we keep our scientists busy creating ingenious ways of killing off people in other nations when we disagree with their leaders?

Like others all over the world, we welcomed the Intermediate-range Nuclear Treaty (INF) signed by Reagan and Gorbachev in December 1987. It offers a *four percent* reduction of the deadly nuclear arsenal of our two nations. It was an important first step toward halting the arms race. But did you hear any suggestion by the U.S. government that reducing nuclear arms by four percent lets us lower the military budget by four percent? Quite the contrary! The Pentagon promptly demanded increases for conventional weapons.

> We have grasped the mystery of the atom and rejected the Sermon on the Mount. Ours is a world of nuclear giants and ethical infants. We know more about killing than we do about living.
>
> Omar Bradley
> General, U.S. Army

And this is understandable. As long as the generals and admirals throughout the globe have the responsibility for protecting their nations through military clout, *we are still stuck in a war system.* We still think in narrow national terms. We must begin to think in planetary terms if we are to achieve our ultimate human right.

At least 16 nations today already have what *Time* magazine has called "the poor man's atomic bomb." Today's nerve gas can produce fever and uncontrolled vomiting that will be followed by paralysis and death by asphyxiation.

> *The splitting of the atom has changed everything, save our mode of thinking, and thus we drift toward unparalleled catastrophe.*
>
> Albert Einstein

According to the American Chemical Association, the Pentagon already has five thousand times enough nerve gas to kill everyone on earth. Other nations may be able to match the U.S. sniff by sniff.

But let's be superoptimists and suppose that a miracle of disarmament happens. Let's imagine that all nations on earth strip themselves of all armaments—*both nuclear and conventional*—and these are completely destroyed by the end of this century. Will humanity now be safe?

No! The technological information that enables us to build efficient killing machines cannot be destroyed. When the people who engineered this hypothetical disarmament miracle are *no longer in office,* politicians with less goodwill (or more hunger for power) could easily reactivate the arms race. If only one nation with a power-mad dictator begins a new arms race, other nations have to "defend" themselves by following suit.

More Guns Won't Work

As we pointed out in the Preface, many sincere people think we'll be safe if we arm to the teeth under the theory of deterrence—often called "mutual assured destruction" (MAD). However, as Emery Reves reminded us, *one person's deterrence is another's in* *centive to start an arms race!* That's what happened to the U.S. and the Soviet Union after World War II.*

Since a nuclear missile can travel anywhere on earth in about 30 minutes, the warning time is now so short that it is possible for a war to be started by a computer malfunction that is misinterpreted. Computers and warning systems have been known to give false alarms. Space debris such as meteors or satellites reentering the atmosphere can be mistaken for a missile attack— especially when tension is high. Do you want the life of your family to terminate because of a computer error?

Fanatics, terrorists, or superpatriots may initiate an unauthorized attack. "An officer for the Navy Department," reports Ted Weiss of the U.S. House of Representatives, "informed me that with the support of as few as three other officers, the Commander of a Trident submarine could launch an unauthorized attack. . . ." This vulnerability probably applies to armed services of other nations throughout the world.

> *Betting on deterrence to continue to save us from nuclear annihilation is like building your house on the side of a volcano and hoping it will never erupt.*
>
> Tom A. Hudgens
> *Let's Abolish War*

When we rely on killing machines, absolute security for one nation must mean absolute insecurity for all the rest. Year by year the increasing proliferation of armaments, and the training of men and women to kill each other, encourages a more and more violent world.

* Emery Reves is the author of *The Anatomy of Peace*, published in the United States in 1945 and translated into more than 20 languages. Half a million copies were sold, and Albert Einstein called the book *the* answer to the political problems raised by the atomic bomb. It brilliantly explains how world peace can only come from world law. Appendix 3 presents his reply to objections that have been raised to getting rid of international anarchy by establishing world government.

8

Poor Third World nations may not be able to afford food, education, or health care, but they've got lots of guns. More guns will not help us achieve planethood.

War Without a Winner

This is not a book on nuclear horror. We do not wish to belabor the peril in which humanity finds itself today. We must, however, present one more overview before we proceed with the **eight positive steps** that you can begin taking immediately to move toward a new era of planethood in which we no longer use killing machines to solve disagreements between nations.

Since Hiroshima, military power isn't what it used to be. World War II was the last major war that will ever be "won" by superior power. There can be no winner in a nuclear war—both sides lose—and lose everything. Scientist

> *The ideology of deterrence must not receive the church's blessing, even as a temporary warrant for holding on to nuclear weapons.*
> Pastoral Letter of
> Methodist Bishops, 1986

Carl Sagan has pointed out that if either the U.S. or the Soviet Union launches an all-out first strike with nuclear missiles, *and the other side does not fire back a single shot in retaliation,* the nuclear winter effect causing the lowering of planetary light and temperature and other lethal consequences will wipe out human life not only in the targeted nation but also in the aggressor nation and throughout most of the earth!!!*

Environmental Ruin

Scientists from all over the world agree that we are rapidly making Planet Earth unsuitable for continued

* *The Cold and the Dark: The World After Nuclear War* by Paul R. Ehrlich, Carl Sagan, Donald Kennedy, Walter Orr Roberts. New York: W.W. Norton & Company, 1984.

9

human life.   Rear Admiral Gene LaRocque, U.S. Navy
(Ret.), tells us:

> The pursuit of military power has gravely under-
> mined another element of overall security: the sound,
> healthy environment necessary to sustain life on this
> planet. In building and maintaining its massive armed
> forces, the United States has created widespread en-
> vironmental problems at home and abroad. . . .
> From the end of World War II through the
> runaway military spending of the Reagan presidency,
> the United States' race to possess more and deadlier
> weapons overwhelmed the concern for a cleaner
> and safer world. The U.S. military establishment has
> either ignored or obtained exemptions from laws
> such as the Resource Conservation and Recovery Act
> and the Clean Water Act that set environmental and
> public health and safety standards for private indus-
> tries, individuals, and municipalities in the United
> States. The majority of U.S. military facilities do not
> meet federal and state hazardous waste control
> requirements.*

Our industries, our lifestyles, and our military activities have already created such damage that we are
today noticing the beginning of the end (breaks in the ozone layer, global warming, water shortages, increasing deserts, overpopulation, disturbances of the delicately balanced

> *This is our world, and it's the only one we've got. We can make these next ten years the 'decade of the environment' or the 'decade of demise.' Which will it be? You can make the difference.*
>
> Diane MacEachern
> *Save Our Planet:*
> *750 Everyday Ways You*
> *Can Help Clean Up the Earth*

chain of life, and on and on). The planetary repair
bill will amount to untold trillions of dollars.   Lester
R. Brown of the Worldwatch Institute advises us,
". . . investing some $150 billion per year in areas that

* From *The Defense Monitor,* Vol. XVIII, No. 6, published by The
Center for Defense Information, 1500 Massachusetts Avenue NW,
Washington, DC 20005.

broaden human options in the face of enormous uncertainty would be a reasonable down payment on an environmentally sustainable global economy."

It is increasingly obvious that we must rapidly globalize our thinking to enable our children to live on Planet Earth.

Crimes Against Humanity

The Nuremberg tribunals condemned aggression and crimes against humanity and ruled that even heads of state were punishable after fair trial before an international court. These principles were unanimously affirmed by the United Nations in 1945. War crimes, including the use of poison gas, have been illegal since 1899. To be sure, hypocritical failure to honor or enforce legal requirements has its price. Failure to punish criminals encourages more criminality.

Let aggressors know that they will face trial and let an international criminal tribunal be created quickly. The blueprints are at hand. The United Nations is considering an International Criminal Court to deal with drug-traffickers, terrorists, and other international criminals. Unfortunately, the United States—the moving spirit behind Nuremberg—has failed to give it support. Would it not be better than unilateral military action, which risks spilling the blood of countless young people?

The only sure way to give you, your family, and all of us a future on this earth (plus unparalleled abundance) is to rapidly achieve a new international system in which *we fight our battles in the courtroom instead of the killing fields*. And this is the central message of *PlanetHood*: we can and must internationally replace the **law of force** with the **force of law.** The Eight Steps in this book will show you how you can help it happen soon.

11

Common sense tells us that if the mortal mind is able to invent ways to destroy the world, it must also be capable of devising a world system to prevent its destruction.

> But the hard fact remains that the decision-making system in the world body is too flawed to deal with the awesome gamut of our planet's problems in the coming decades. It is neither morally right or politically sensible to leave veto power in the Security Council in the hands of the five nuclear powers. It is plainly absurd to have decisions made on the basis of one nation, one vote in the General Assembly, thus giving countries with minute populations and minuscule contributions to the U.N. budget the same influence in decision-making as the bigger countries that have to pay the bills. Moreover, a central global decision-making body that can pass only non-binding recommendations is not what the world needs for the 21st century.
>
> Richard Hudson
> *Global Report*
> Center for War/Peace Studies

Optimism and individual effort are essential if the problems of human survival are to be solved. Without optimism that human betterment is possible, despondency and despair would destroy the initiative and determination that are needed to defeat the prophecies of doom. Hope is the motor that drives human endeavor. Only through confidence in the future can humankind muster the courage and strength to do what is required for survival. We have, therefore, deliberately chosen to view the glass as half full rather than half empty.

But we are also convinced that *optimism is justified by the facts.* Despite all the contemporary stresses and strife, the historical record shows that humankind is experiencing a continuous—though wobbly—movement toward a more cooperative world order. The growth described in this book must be nurtured with care if it is to reach maturity. *We must not be tempted to abandon the baby just because it was not born full grown.*

Our Ultimate Human Right

The time has come for "we the people" to prevent our own annihilation. Let us proclaim an ultimate human right that can act as a rallying call:

I have the right to live with dignity in a healthy environment free from the threat of war.

We must strongly assert our ultimate human right in ways that our military and political leaders can hear— firmly, caringly, and *nonviolently.* To fall into the trap of violence in the cause of nonviolence and peace is simply perpetuating the old habits of thinking that have put us into our present predicament.

The people on this earth do not want to be killed through nuclear war—or any other kind of war. Mothers, fathers, and children have suffered far too much from the recurrent wars that have plagued human history for thousands of years.

> *Unless some effective supranational government can be set up and brought quickly into action, the prospects of peace and human progress are dark and doubtful.*
>
> Winston Churchill
> British Prime Minister

Unfortunately when many of these same people acquire positions of military and political power in the governments of the world, they fall into the trap of thinking that killing power equals national success. Today this is small-brain dinosaur thinking.

The First Step you can take to rescue yourself from extinction is to clearly assert your *ultimate human right* to live with dignity in a healthy environment free from the threat of war. This right is called "ultimate," for unless we can make the transition from the *law of force* to the *force of law*, all our other rights will remain in jeopardy. Our rights to practice the faith of our choice; to earn a living; and to have decent housing, food, medical care, and the "pursuit of happiness" are *meaningless* if there are no human beings on earth to enjoy these rights! Whatever religious, economic, social, political, or other benefits we wish to enjoy, all will be lost unless we rapidly secure our *ultimate human right.*

> *It is high time for humanity to accept and work out the full consequences of the total global and interdependent nature of our planetary home and of our species. Our survival and further progress will depend largely on the advent of global visions and of proper global education in all countries of the world.*
>
> Robert Muller, 1982
> Author and U.N. Assistant
> Secretary-General

It's Your Birthright

This proclamation of our basic human right is not something invented out of thin air. It has been developing as part of the growing respect for the rights of all individuals. *This ultimate human right, upon which all other human rights depend, can only be protected by replacing international lawlessness with enforced international law.*

The United Nations Charter confirms the determination of all nations "to save succeeding generations from the scourge of war." The Universal Declaration of Human Rights adopted in 1948 by the U.N. declares that "everyone has the right to life, liberty and security of person" and refers to "a social order and international order" in which those rights "can be fully realized." These civil, political, economic, social, and cultural rights have been promised to all humankind by the United Nations.

14

Without peace, no human right is secure. The monetary and human cost of preparing for war (usually called "defense") makes it impossible to fully attain our declared human rights. The costs of preserving our environment and providing clean air and water can only be met by cutting the crushing burden of militarism.

This constant threat of warfare places all living things in mortal peril. It is appropriate, therefore, that the ultimate human right be clearly articulated

> *Peace through strength is a fallacy. . . . The national defense of this Nation has left us vulnerable, but not because we lack an arsenal. . . . Our vulnerability is the people who are without homes, nutrition, education, health care. Ultimately, the security of the Nation is not found in its materialism. It is found in a spirit. It is found in a strength of heart and mind. It is found in its people—we the people.*
> Senator Mark O. Hatfield
> Oregon Republican
> Congressional Record, 1989

and proclaimed as the supreme goal for the remaining years of the 20th Century. The guardian of all of our hopes, dreams, and truths resides in our ultimate human right to live with dignity in a healthy environment free from the threat of war.

Your First Step Toward Planethood

Your First Step toward planethood is to assert your ultimate right as a human being who shares our common planet. We hope a proclamation of the ultimate human right will be signed by every concerned citizen throughout the world. It should be posted on the walls of our offices and factories, made visually available in every home, printed on billboards, taught in every school, and written in the sky.

Appendix 4 contains copies of this proclamation you can duplicate and use in signing up your friends and neighbors. When each sheet is filled out, it should be sent to Mr. Javier Pérez de Cuéllar, Secretary-General of the United Nations, with a request that he inform the nations of the world what we, the people, are demanding. You can begin to let people know you're fed up with the way the world is being run.

As we mentioned, there are Eight Steps YOU can take to help make this ultimate human right a living reality for yourself and everyone. In the following pages, we will outline what many years of intensive study tell us will work. We offer it only as a frame of reference. Others may approach the problems of human survival from a different perspective. We welcome that. The more people ponder these vital problems, the sooner wise solutions will be found.

> *Ask not what your country can do for you, ask what you can do for your country.*
> John F. Kennedy
> U.S. President

By taking this first step, you are beginning to insist on your ultimate human right. You are now ready to consider the Second Step (explained in the next section) to secure your right to live with dignity in a healthy environment free from the threat of war—and to benefit by the exciting new era the 21st Century offers us.

2nd Step

Understand What Needs to Be Done

There'll always be a bad guy hanging out in the international neighborhood as long as we have an ungoverned world of anarchy and lawlessness. This book describes a sure way to save humanity from the perpetual warfare that squeezes us to pay for killing machines and deprives us of planetary prosperity—and the

> *We have a choice. Humanity either can learn to manage the risks of living together under a law system or can prepare to die together under the war system.*
> Myron W. Kronisch
> Campaign for U.N. Reform

funds needed to preserve our environment. And it's realistic and practical. It doesn't depend on everyone's becoming nice and kind by tomorrow!

Unless we change our ways, humanity seems headed toward eventual death. Some new approach is needed to give our children a future! How do we switch from the arms race to a peace and prosperity race? What can we do about the gravest environmental crisis humanity has ever faced?

Solving the Problem of War

The only way to permanently solve the problem of war between nations is to replace the LAW OF FORCE with the FORCE OF LAW.

Laying aside all the jokes we love to tell about our politicians, *we've developed systems for governing ourselves that really work!* You probably slept soundly in your bed last night because your city has a system

19

of laws, enforcement, and courts that make you relatively safe. (Bear in mind nothing's perfect—we are talking about practicalities.)

Similarly, the state in which you live has a political structure that provides the three elements needed for adequate government: elected state representatives to make laws; an executive branch with police to enforce the laws; and state courts

> . . . they shall beat their swords into plowshares, and their spears into pruning hooks: nations shall not lift up a sword against nation, neither shall they learn war any more.
>
> The Bible, Micah 4:3

to fairly resolve disputes, decide who's innocent, who's broken the law, and what their punishment will be.

Without these three elements—*laws, courts, and enforcement*—lawlessness would reign. Without their protection, you might have to kill or risk being killed just to provide yourself with a lower level of safety than your city, county, and state governments are now giving you. Remember the Wild West of the last century in which anyone with a pistol could act as a lawmaker, enforcer, judge, jury, and executioner—sometimes all within one minute?

In the Wild West, people wore guns on their hips to "protect" themselves. Any barroom dispute could end in killing. Outlaws ran wild. The death rate without law and order was much too high. To create peaceful communities, the citizens demanded sheriffs and courts to enforce laws—not just every man for himself. We must now do this internationally. As we did in the Wild West, we can take the pistols off separate national belts and put them on an international sheriff.

A workable alternative to the use of force requires many innovations. The United Nations must be altered to provide us with an international congress to make laws and a court system to settle disputes. An International Peace Force must be created as the ultimate law enforcement agency so that each country will not need its own army, navy, and air force for national security. We can and must develop a system of mutual security that protects all nations under international law.

Those who are expected to comply with international law and order must be convinced that the laws are as fair as can be expected. They must recognize that the objective of the system is not the exploitation of the weak or the preservation of privilege for the powerful. No system of law can be enforced if it does not have as its most vital ingredient the goal of social justice for the entire human community.*

> *Abolition of war is no longer an ethical question to be pondered solely by learned philosophers and ecclesiastics, but a hard core one for the decision of the masses whose survival is the issue. Many will tell you with mockery and ridicule that the abolition of war can only be a dream . . . that it is the vague imagining of a visionary. But we must go on or we will go under! We must have new thoughts, new ideas, new concepts. We must break out of the straitjacket of the past. We must have sufficient imaginations and courage to translate the universal wish for peace—which is rapidly becoming a universal necessity—into actuality.*
>
> Douglas MacArthur
> General, U.S. Army

Just One More Layer of Law

Today in the United States, we have four layers of government: city, county, state, and national. We have these four layers because we need them to avoid anarchy *within our nation.* It's inspiring to know that *adding*

---

* All of this is spelled out in *Enforcing International Law—A Way to World Peace* by Benjamin B. Ferencz. 2 volumes. New York: Oceana Publications, 1983. Available in many university libraries.

only one more level of government will enable us to have an abundant future on this planet.

International governance—something like a United Nations of the World—will rescue us from our deadly predicament. U.S. President Harry S. Truman in his down-to-earth way said, "When Kansas and Colorado have a quarrel over water in the Arkansas River, they don't call out the National Guard in each state and go to war over it. They bring suit in the Supreme Court of the United States and abide by the decision. There isn't a reason in the world why we cannot do that internationally. . . . It will be just as easy for nations to get along in a republic of the world as it is for you to get along in the republic of the United States."

The gradual growth of international law and cooperation over the past century has set the stage for us to create a permanent peace with worldwide prosperity. Let's look at the progress we have made in replacing the *law of force* with the *force of law.* Louis Sohn, professor of international law, emeritus, Harvard Law School, has pointed out that in the last

> . . . forty years more international agreements have been concluded than during the previous four millennia; that the International Court of Justice after a period of unemployment has now more cases than it can comfortably handle (including several cases testifying to its acceptance by the African countries and other new members of the international community); that several regional and functional courts are dealing with a rapidly increasing number of cases; and that more than two hundred international organizations deal with matters of daily concern to the majority of mankind in such an efficient and smooth way that their activities are generally accepted without a murmur.*

* From Professor Sohn's Introduction to *A Common Sense Guide to World Peace* by Benjamin B. Ferencz. New York: Oceana Publications, 1985.

This progress can now become a foundation for a lawful world. You'll be amazed at how much has already been done. According to Willy Brandt, former chancellor of West Germany, "The Federal Republic of Germany [in becoming a member of the European Community] has declared in its Constitution its

> *Mankind's desire for peace can be realized only by the creation of a world government.*
> Albert Einstein

willingness to transfer sovereign rights to supernational organizations and it has placed international law above national law. . . . This expresses the realization that the sovereignty of the individual and of nations can be secured only in larger communities."

Many other constitutions and treaties drawn up in recent years provide for some subordination of national government to an international system of law and order. Among these are the constitutions of Belgium, France, Costa Rica, India, Italy, Japan, Luxembourg, and Norway.

After World War II, General Douglas MacArthur insisted that the 1947 Japanese Constitution prohibit Japan from maintaining land, sea, and air forces in the future. Article Nine states that Japan " . . . forever renounces war as a sovereign right of a nation, and the threat or use of force as means of settling international disputes." That restraint enabled Japan to concentrate on rebuilding its economy—and to become one of the most influential nations in the world. Power does not depend upon armies—but on people.

To give ourselves the peace and abundance of planethood, *we must enlarge our idea of patriotism.* George Washington also faced the problem of limited loyalty. For example, during the war for American independence one woman wrote, "Washington tried

> *This statement is for all those who fear that it is unpatriotic to have a government greater than their own. There is no greater patriotic duty than to preserve your own nation and its freedoms. It is true that we must retain our freedoms when we unite into one federation, except for the freedom to make war. Just as our own 50 states have turned over this task to our national government, so the 160 nations, or however many join, must turn over warmaking and defense to the world federation. I live in Cherry Hills, Colorado, and I think it is the finest city in the world. I live in Arapahoe County, and I think it is the finest county in the world. I live in the state of Colorado, and I think it is the greatest state in the world. I live in the United States of America, and I think it is the greatest country in the world. But I also live on Planet Earth, and it does not detract one iota from my patriotism to my city, my county, my state, and my country for me to feel that this planet is the greatest in the universe and that I will defend it against all perils to the best of my ability. What we need in this world is a pledge of allegiance to Planet Earth by every citizen of the world.*
>
> Tom A. Hudgens
> *Let's Abolish War*

to persuade his New Jersey troops to swear allegiance to the United States. They refused. 'New Jersey is our country!' they said stubbornly." In the Continental Congress a New Jersey member denounced the General's action as improper.

Our patriotism must be enlarged one more step to the international level for the common good of all humanity. If we work as hard to promote a world republic as we do to sell cola drinks in every country, we can achieve a lawful world free from the threat of war before the end of this century. *PlanetHood* is an idea whose time has come.

International "Wild West" Must End

Today no world legislature exists to legally define what each country may or may not do. There is no executive branch to enforce international laws, and no world court makes *binding* decisions based on an international constitution. As matters now stand, nations decide for themselves how to handle conflicts. They pick which versions of ambiguous agreements they will follow.

Many agreements have been accepted by the world community to stipulate the bounds of permissible international behavior. But almost all such instruments contain artfully constructed clauses *deliberately formulated with such skillful ambiguity* as to allow each nation to interpret the vague phrases to its advantage! *Any system that allows competing parties to interpret laws primarily on the basis of their own advantage is unworthy of respect.* It is practically no legal system at all!

> *Internationalism does not mean the end of individual nations. Orchestras don't mean the end of violins.*
> Golda Meir
> Prime Minister of Israel

In 1979, for example, 118 nations voted for the International Convention Against the Taking of Hostages. Any party apprehending an offender was obliged "without exception whatsoever" to prosecute or extradite the criminal. Despite this seemingly comprehensive language, exceptions were put in that gave sanctuary to those who acted for political motives or who were fighting against "colonial domination and alien occupation" or "in the exercise of their right of self-determination." The same loopholes appeared in agreements against other acts of terrorism. Under such circumstances of legal double talk, it should surprise no one that acts of terrorism have continued.

The definition of aggression is so riddled with contradictory clauses that it is all but ignored by the Security Council of the United Nations, which is supposed to be guided by it. Binding treaties, signed to keep the skies free of ballistic missiles, are later interpreted in ways that defeat the fundamental purposes of the agreement.

> *We are convinced that a comprehensive system of security is at the same time a system of universal law and order ensuring the primacy of international law in politics . . . .*
>
> Mikhail Gorbachev
> Soviet General Secretary
> Article in *Pravda*
> September 17, 1987

If laws are designed with loopholes, international lawbreakers will use the loopholes to do as they please. Those who wish to live under the protection of law cannot be allowed to evade the law through self-serving misinterpretations.

Three Alternatives

A planetary system must be set up so that it is *not too powerful* (thus avoiding tyranny) *and not too weak* (thus avoiding ineffectiveness). There are three basic ways to create a system of international governance—ranging from bad to good:

1. **A World Dictatorship.** An awful way to get rid of world anarchy is to set up a world system with a powerful world dictator or international king of all countries. The history of dictators like Hitler warns us that *power must be limited.* Lord Acton in 1887 observed, "Power tends to corrupt; absolute power corrupts absolutely." Strong checks and balances are essential to prevent concentrated power in the hands of one person—or one special interest. A world dictatorship is definitely *not* the solution we are seeking; it would be like jumping out of the frying pan into the fire.

2. **A Confederation of Nations.** A confederation sounds good on paper, but in practice it just doesn't

work. The United Nations today is a confederation of 160 sovereign nations. With good intentions its Charter begins, "We the Peoples of the United Nations determined to save succeeding generations from the scourge of war . . . ." The U.N. has a General Assembly (in which each nation has one vote), a Security Council, and a World Court at The Hague. Unfortunately, like our Articles of Confederation written over two centuries ago, the Charter can't work to reliably prevent wars because it's too weak.

> One reason nations go to war (there are 40 wars now going on around the world) is because at times they have no other place to go. Contending parties can become so locked into rigid positions that squaring off in blood seems the only alternative.
>
> Eric Cox
> Campaign for U.N. Reform

Today's U.N. is still stuck in a war system! When Iran grabbed the American Embassy and held its people as hostages, the U.S. went to the World Court at The Hague. It decided unanimously in favor of the U.S. *However, there was no enforcement of the court decision!* So the hostages remained prisoners.

Most nations, including the United States, have not hesitated to ignore international law. Bill Moyers reminds us that unmarked planes flown by CIA pilots have bombed the Guatemalan capital. When the United States mined a Nicaraguan harbor and Nicaragua filed a complaint, the U.S. rejected the Court's jurisdiction. World protests were ignored when Soviet troops were sent to Afghanistan. The usual anarchy attitude is: *either accept our illegal actions—or go to war with us.*

The Charter was deliberately made weak so that no one could tell anyone else what to do. We made it impotent, and—by giving five powerful nations the right to veto any enforcement action—*we deliberately left open the option of settling disputes by war.* In spite of the high ideals in the Charter and its prohibition against the use of force (except in self-defense), we did not give the United Nations the binding strength needed to get rid of international lawlessness.

The U.N. has, however, been a valuable and necessary step in setting the stage for a more workable international governance. It's now time to reform the U.N. into an effective vehicle for peaceful planethood.

3. A World Democratic Republic. We know that a world dictatorship or a global confederation or league won't work to solve international anarchy. Here's what will work: a democratic republic of the world that can complete our governmental structure to get rid of international lawlessness.

All nations on the earth can be protected by an international constitution providing for an international congress to pass laws, an international court to apply the laws, and an international executive branch to enforce the laws. Our representatives to the world congress would protect us in a way that we lack today. We can achieve our "planethood" through a United Nations of the world—just as we achieved our nationhood through the Constitution of the United States of America.*

Power Must Be Limited by Law

We must *limit the power* of a world system in the way our Founding Fathers limited the power of the

* See *World Peace Through World Law* by Grenville Clark and Louis B. Sohn. 3rd ed. Cambridge: Harvard University Press, 1966. A basic book describing reforms needed to make the U.N. effective.

United States Government. We must use checks and balances to avoid the pitfalls of power. We must provide the people of the world with peace and dignity through international law enforced by an executive branch and a world judiciary.

The U.S. Constitution left power in the hands of the individual states and the people. The U.S. government was given only the minimum power needed for the effective operation of the federal government; for example, to deal with interstate or international matters. Disagreements between states are settled legally—not lethally—by U.S. laws, courts, and executive enforcement. *Because of the wise checks and balances that limit the power of Congress, the Supreme Court, and the executive branch, no king or dictator can get control of the government of the United States.*

To save all of humanity from extinction and set the stage for worldwide prosperity and environmental sustainability, we can use a governmental structure similar to the one that for over two centuries has made the United States one of the most prosperous and strongest nations on earth. U.S. citizens are given enormous individual rights—bearing in mind that my right to swing my arms freely ends where your nose begins! We have a successful model that can work in the international area just as it has worked for the United States in the national area.

> *I have long believed the only way peace can be achieved is through World Government.*
> Jawaharal Nehru
> Former Prime Minister of India

Safely Disarming!

When we are protected by international laws, courts, and effective enforcement, we can AT LAST safely disarm this bristling world. This would include destroying all

ESSENTIALS OF A
WORLD CONSTITUTION

1. A Bill of Rights.
2. A popularly elected legislature to enact world laws.
3. A world court to interpret those laws, with compulsory jurisdiction over world disputes.
4. A civilian executive branch with the power to enforce world laws directly upon individuals.
5. A system of checks and balances to prevent the abuse of power by any branch of the world government.
6. The control of all weapons of mass destruction by the world government, with the disarmament of all nations, under careful inspection down to the level required for internal policing.
7. Carefully defined and limited power of taxation to support those functions necessary to world peace and the solution of problems affecting, to a vital degree, the welfare of all mankind.
8. Reasonable provision for amendments.
9. Participation in the world federal government to be open at all times to all nations.
10. All power not expressly delegated to the world government to be reserved to the nations and their peoples, thus leaving each nation to choose its own political, social, and economic systems.

Other Constitutions have been drafted by other organizations. The ultimate form should be hammered out by an international constitutional convention.

From the American Movement for World Government, One World Trade Center, Suite 7967, New York, NY 10048.

mass killing machines. *Those deadly bombers, missiles, tanks, submarines, and battleships are not needed to maintain law and order inside a nation.* No more armies, navies, air forces, or Star Wars! No international arms trade. They wouldn't be needed.

The United Nations would instead have a staff of well-trained and equipped air and ground peacekeeping forces to keep order among the nation-states of the world. Think of all the money and lives this would save! Instead of many millions of soldiers in national armies *which have not kept world order*, a few hundred thousand world "policemen" could preserve planetary law and order. And the price is right!

> *I am convinced that the Great Framer of the World will so develop it that it becomes one nation, so that armies and navies are no longer necessary . . . . I believe at some future day, the nations of the earth will agree upon some sort of congress which will take cognizance of international questions of difficulty and whose decisions will be as binding as the decisions of our Supreme Court are upon us.*
>
> Ulysses S. Grant
> U.S. President, 1869–1877

National Rights Protected

We don't want the ways of other nations forced on us, and we must understandably avoid trying to push our economic, social, religious, or political forms on other countries. The U.S. Constitution wisely limits the power of the federal government to interfere with matters inside a state. Similarly a world constitution must allow the people of the world to run their own countries. Each nation could determine for itself how to run its own economy and politics. The goal is international unity—not national uniformity. Unity with diversity!

While the reformed United Nations organization would have a democratic voting system and the right

31

to pass binding laws, the 160 individual nation-states would continue to choose their own forms of government. Thus, Saudi Arabia has a king; some countries may have presidents that were not elected by the people; England has a parliamentary system based on both heredity and popular vote; Sweden and Iceland could remain socialistic; and some countries will have federated states like the United States. If individual nations wish to hold onto or change their way of governing themselves, it's their own business.

> The basic reason for the frustration of efforts to disarm is that disarmament negotiations have sought to treat the symptoms of the arms race—military forces—rather than the underlying cause of the arms race—the failure of our small planet to create an alternative problem-solving system on which nations can rely for their safety. Nations have felt the need for armed forces for centuries, and it is altogether too much to ask them to disarm in a political vacuum. If they lay down their arms, how do they provide for their security?
>
> Richard Hudson, Director
> Center for War/Peace Studies

The international peacekeeping forces and the World Court would have the power to stop any nation from illegally using armed force or military threats to coerce the people of any other nation in any way at any time in any form. Grievances could be brought before the World Court, whose decisions would be binding. An international congress, a World Court, and the enforcement branch would keep the nations of the world *far safer in preserving their traditions than they are today.* There is no safety in today's world. Through enforced world law, all nations would be safe!

Can a nation try to convince other nations to do as it does? Yes. Using the international right of free speech guaranteed by the world constitution, the U.S. will be free to try to convince other nations to adopt its political and economic forms; Sweden and Iceland can try to persuade other nations to adopt a socialistic economy. However, invading another country to impose one's own government is an illegal act of aggression that would not be tolerated.

On Toward Planethood

The world today is one big neighborhood. International problems such as air, land, and ocean pollution, disease control, the use of natural resources, and terrorism require international solutions. Two centuries ago, if you got on a stagecoach at 3:00 in the morning and rode until 10:00 that night, you could average 40 miles per day—in good weather! Computer networks, fax, telephones, radio, and TV have shrunk the globe. Using jet planes you can travel

> *You cannot erect a peace system on a basis of the coercion of governments by governments, because that is trying to build a peace system on a foundation of war. The only basis for a peace system is a pooling of sovereignty for supernational purposes, that is the creation of a common nationhood, above but entirely separate from the diverse local nationhoods.*
>
> Philip Henry Kerr
> Marquis of Lothian
> Burge Memorial Lecture, 1935

anywhere in hours. With satellite TV communication today, you can hear and see events all over the world as though they were next door.

Even if humanity's future were not in jeopardy, a new world system is essential to the unfolding of a bountiful life for our children. Suppose the United States were broken up into fifty sovereign, separate nations. To drive from San Francisco to New York on Interstate Highway 80, (assuming there was an I-80), you'd have to stop and submit to customs and immigration procedures in twelve different countries! And you might have to exchange your money a dozen times to buy things in each separate nation-state. This would enormously reduce the wonderful vitality that the United States has developed as one nation.

> *Science has made unrestricted national sovereignty incompatible with human survival. The only possibilities are now world government or death.*
> Bertrand Russell
> Philosopher

In a recent trade agreement, both the U.S. and Canada recognized that the old system of trade barriers makes little sense in the modern world.

International Coordination

When the 160 nations of earth are united into an international system, every aspect of our lives will be greatly enriched—to say nothing of the hundreds of billions of dollars each year that will be transferred from killing machines to more abundant living. We can create a new era with new business opportunities, broader education, increased health care, and greater cultural richness. This is what *PlanetHood* is about.

Twelve independent European nations with a long history of fratricidal wars have recognized the need to surrender part of their sovereignty as a price for peace and prosperity. They are Germany, France, Italy, Belgium, the Netherlands, Luxembourg, Denmark, Ireland, Greece, Spain, Portugal, and the United Kingdom. This European Community will create a "single market" by December 31, 1992. Common economic norms and standards will be established in a "Europe without frontiers."

Jean Monnet, the architect of European unity, proclaimed, "We are not forming coalitions between states, but union among people." Freedom from import taxes and trade barriers will let trade flow as freely among the 12 European nation-states as between New York and Pennsylvania in the United States of America. There will be tariffs on imports from nonmember nations.

Labor, capital, goods, and services can move freely within the European Community nations. The 12 national currencies will be replaced by the single ECU—European Currency Unit. An open door will invite other countries to join the European Community. Probably many Eastern European nations and perhaps Russia will eventually join. The stage is set for unparalleled freedom and prosperity.

The European Council, Parliament, and Court of Justice now operating will build a better future for 320 million Europeans in one of the world's largest trading blocks. The community has a flag—12 gold stars in a field of blue, and the community anthem is Beethoven's *Ode to Joy!* And all this can pave the way to eventually replace 12 sets of war machines with a single mutual security system. A mini-version of planethood will then have arrived in Europe!

What is valid for twelve European nations is also valid for all other nation-states. Cooperative international management will benefit everyone.

The Eight Steps explained in this book give you ways you can help create a world free from

> All mankind would be grateful for all time to the statesman who could bring about a new structure of international society.
>
> Theodore Roosevelt
> U.S. President
> Upon accepting the
> Nobel Peace Prize, 1910

war and want. In the First Step, we stressed the importance of asserting our ultimate human right: to live with dignity in a healthy environment free from the threat of war. The Second Step requires that we understand what needs to be done: create a world system with international laws, courts, and enforcement—and then safely and permanently disarm all nations.

By thus achieving our planethood, the present international "Wild West" anarchy will become a colorful historical memory. We will have met the challenge of our time—and won! Our children will have a greater future than any generation that has walked on this earth: freed from the costly arms race and with environmental protection based on enforceable international law, the people of this earth will enjoy safer and richer lives as we join hands together to greet the 21st Century in planetary unity.

> *We should strive for greater effectiveness and efficiency of the United Nations. The United States is committed to playing its part in helping to maintain global security, promoting democracy and prosperity.*
>
> George Bush
> U.S. President, October 1, 1990
> Address to the United Nations

3rd Step

*Become a
Planethood
Patriot*

The Third Step will show you how to become a planethood patriot. You will actually learn how to follow in George Washington's footsteps and be- come a modern founder of law and order—throughout the world. Step 3 will add to your insight and determination to do the job that must be done to save humanity.

In 1776 the American colonies wanted indepen- dence from England.

> The popular notion about the origin of the United States gov- ernment is that the Declaration of Independence and the United States Constitution were part of a single historical process. There were years of disintegration and deterioration after the end of the Revolution. The United States was not born in 1776 with the Declaration of Independence but in 1787 when the U.S. Constitu- tion came into being.
>
> Norman Cousins, President
> World Federalist Association

Under the leadership of General George Washington, we fought the Revolutionary War and defeated England, and the United States of America was off and running as a great nation. Right? No, wrong!

Except for a few students of history, most people do not realize that after the colonies won the War of Independence from England, there was no government of the United States of America. There were only thirteen sovereign nation-states. They got together to draft the "Articles of Confederation and Perpetual Union" to set forth the ground rules for relating to each other.

The First Attempt

Although completed on November 15, 1777, it took five years for all the thirteen nation-states to agree to sign the Articles of Confederation and Perpetual Union. Under the Articles, the nation-states agreed not to make alliances or treaties or set up separate embassies in any foreign nation, not to enter into treaties between themselves without the agreement of the other states, and not to keep any military or naval force except militia needed for internal order. At least nine states had to vote in favor of a major law for it to pass. To make any changes in the Articles, all the states had to agree unanimously.

However, the limited cooperation that existed during the war soon began to evaporate in peacetime. Agreements under the Articles were often ignored when it pleased a state to do so. Under the Articles of Confederation, there was no executive leader, the Continental Congress did not have the power to make enforceable laws, and no court had the power to settle disputes between the states.

> *The primary cause of all disorders lies in the different state governments and in the tenacity of that power which pervades the whole of their systems.*
>
> George Washington

There was no way to pay for confederation expenses except by asking the states to contribute their share. Just as the United States is now doing with the United Nations, the nation-states petulantly chose to cut off funds when things didn't go the way they wanted. "By 1786," according to John Fiske in *The Critical Period of American History 1783–1789*, "under the universal depression and want of confidence, all trade had wellnigh stopped, and political quackery, with its cheap and dirty remedies, had full control of the field."

The Articles of Confederation did not base the intended government on the vote of the people. Appointment to the Continental Congress, the funding, and the power came through the thirteen state governments, which were concerned with their private interests. The appointed politicians considered that they represented only the interests of each nation-state. Agreements under the Articles of Confederation were usually ignored. Action in critical matters was blocked by the fear of offending or alienating a state; thus wise overall policies or actions to correct violations of the agreed-on Articles were not employed for "strategic" reasons. The only way to enforce the agreements under the Articles of Confederation was by the threat of war. Doesn't this sound like the U.N. today?

Increasing Chaos and Anarchy

Since each of the thirteen nation-states could violate without penalty anything they'd agreed to under the Articles, it is not surprising that the United States of America began falling apart. New York funded a lot of its government expenses with tariffs collected on goods from Connecticut and New Jersey—even though such tariffs were forbidden under the Articles. Every "Yankee" ship and New Jersey market boat had to pay entrance fees and clear New York customs just like ships from London or Hamburg. Boycotting the Congress when a state did not get its way was frequent. The Congress often had too few delegates present to do business, it seldom had money in its bank account, and its credit was shot, so it could not borrow.

It became obvious that, under the Articles, the states had created only a treaty of alliance and a forum for communicating—not a U.S. Government. Since the Continental Congress was totally without the power to enforce anything, it was in effect simply a "town meeting" of the thirteen sovereign nation-states.

Every year things continued to fly apart. The oyster and crab fishermen of Maryland and Virginia were fighting with one another over fishing rights on the Potomac River. Since Pennsylvania and Delaware also used the Potomac for shipping, they added to the heat of the argument. Under the Articles of Confederation, the Continental Congress was powerless to settle the relatively small issue of the "oyster war."

> We hold these truths to be self-evident, that all men are created equal, that they are endowed by their Creator with certain unalienable Rights, that among these are Life, Liberty and the pursuit of Happiness. That to secure these rights, Governments are instituted among Men, deriving their just powers from the consent of the governed. That whenever any Form of Government becomes destructive of these ends, it is the Right of the People to alter or to abolish it, and to institute new Government, laying its foundation on such principles and organizing its powers in such form, as to them shall seem most likely to effect their Safety and Happiness.
>
> Declaration of Independence
> 1776

The peace treaty with England was separately ratified by Virginia in violation of the Articles—as though signing by the Continental Congress was not enough! Some states were borrowing money abroad as if they were separate nations. Nine states from Massachusetts to South Carolina had navies of their own, and all the states considered their militia as state armies.

Under the Articles, Congress had the sole right to provide for coinage, and it had never minted a single U.S. coin! In violation of agreements under the Articles, seven of the states were irresponsibly printing paper money. Since paper money was often worthless, barter was common. Isaiah Thomas, editor of the Worcester *Spy*, announced that you could pay for a subscription to his paper with salt pork.

When Congress in 1781 tried to raise money for its empty treasury by a 5% duty on imported goods, the representatives from New York blocked it because they wanted their own customs system to extract money from the neighboring states. Lacking good ports of its own, New Jersey had to send its exports through New York or Philadelphia

> *There are those who believe that the abolition of war will come only when the hearts of all men are changed to want peace. However, our U.S. government was not formed only after all the people in the thirteen original states had become saints. Instead it was formed to control men of ill will, to set standards by which men could live with one another, encroaching upon each other's freedom as little as possible, and to provide the institutions to settle disputes among states and among people. Our task today is to carry this same concept one level higher, so that a world federation can provide the institutions to settle disputes among nations and among people.*
>
> Tom A. Hudgens
> *Let's Abolish War*

and to pay taxes to both of these states. Benjamin Franklin called New Jersey "a keg tapped at both ends."

Things were a mess. In 1785 Connecticut passed a law that gave its manufacturers and merchants an advantage over industries in New York and Massachusetts. As described by Clarence Streit in *Union Now*, ". . . they lived in a time when New York was protecting its fuel interests by a tariff on Connecticut wood and its farmers by duties on New Jersey butter, when Massachusetts closed while Connecticut opened its ports to British shipping, when Boston was boycotting Rhode Island grain and Philadelphia was refusing to accept New Jersey money, when the money of Connecticut, Delaware and Virginia was sound, that of all other States was variously depreciated and that of Rhode Island and Georgia was so worthless that their governments sought to coerce the citizens into accepting it. In those days New York was massing troops on its Vermont frontier while the Pennsylvania army was committing the atrocities of the 'Wyoming massacre' against settlers from Connecticut." About 2,000 people were killed in this war between Pennsylvania and Connecticut before it was stopped!

In 1786 many people in the New England states were threatening to leave the Union and start their own confederation. No wonder that Vernon Nash wrote in *The World Must Be Governed*, ". . . for fatuous proceedings and a low level of snarling debate to match what we have beheld in the Security Council, one must go to the records of the Continental Congress. That body was of no more consequence than the assemblies in each of our modern leagues [the League of Nations and the United Nations] have been. After the Revolutionary War, the Continental Congress suffered the same fate as our two world forums; respect for it, both at home and abroad, declined to the vanishing point."

> *The value of a citizen's currency would shrink 10 percent when he or she crossed a state line. Thus a citizen who started out from New Hampshire with $100 in his pocket would have $20.24 left by the time he arrived in Georgia—without having spent a cent.*
>
> Norman Cousins
> World Federalist
> Bicentennial Reader

After four years of turmoil in all parts of the country, with troops called out in several states to handle situations and with civil war narrowly avoided at least half a dozen times, the future looked dark. George Washington was deeply concerned that the United States after winning the war would tear itself apart in peace.

He wrote to John Jay in June 1786, "I am uneasy and apprehensive, more so than during the war."

The Constitutional Convention

Disturbed by festering conflicts, Virginia proposed a meeting in Annapolis in September 1786 to discuss the regulation of trade among the states. The delegates were unable to agree on anything except to meet again in Philadelphia on the second Monday of the following May. This turned out to be the famous Constitutional Convention of 1787. The Continental Congress authorized it to meet for "the sole purpose of revising the Articles of Confederation, and reporting to Congress and the several Legislatures, such alterations and provisions therein, as shall, when agreed to in Congress, and confirmed by the states, render the Federal Constitution adequate to the exigencies of Government, and the preservation of the Union."

The delegates faced a seemingly impossible task. They were scared of a king's getting into power and putting them right back where they were before the War of Independence (just as we are scared stiff of setting up a world government that could be seized by a dictator). The thirteen states were also not willing to give up control of their own affairs. And yet they faced conflict and wars the way things were going. The forms of government that had been tried in the history of civilization to that date usually erred on the side of either impotency or tyranny. You can choose your poison—there's no way for the people to win. Or so it seemed.

> *In 1787 a new nation aborning needed unity more than anything else . . . . In 1987, it is the whole world that needs to be united.*
>
> Father Theodore Hesburgh
> Former President
> Notre Dame University

The Founding Fathers of our nation in Philadelphia in the summer of 1787 didn't know how to do it—and yet they knew they had to do it! The biggest problem facing the convention was how to avoid repeating the mistakes of the past. Delegate James Wilson of Pennsylvania observed, "There are two kinds of bad government—the one which does too much and therefore is oppressive, and the other which does too little and therefore is weak."

How do you find the fine line between too much power and too little? How do you preserve each state with its individual uniqueness and yet have an overall power for the common good? How do you balance the rights of minorities and majorities? How do you guarantee individual freedom to the greatest extent consistent with the common good? How do you set things up so fairly that disagreeing people *choose to fight in a court instead of the battlefield?*

> *In the midst of this turmoil, 55 men came together in Philadelphia in the summer of 1787 and drew up a document which provided the framework of government for a nation that became the most successful on earth.*
>
> **The Economist**

They were familiar with the problem of power. The ruthlessness, the ignoring of human rights, the wasting of the people's blood and money on wars had been demonstrated time and time again to be the penalties that are paid for an all-powerful national government. Such dictatorships and monarchies without checks and balances usually enforce their decisions in ways that are not responsive to the wishes of the people. And yet the weak government they had set up under the Articles of Confederation was being ignored at will.

Was there any way out of this dilemma? Was it possible to have a government that could avoid falling into the fatal pits of ineffectiveness or of dictatorship? And if such a government could be formed, how would it interact with existing states? If nation-states were to be controlled by a supreme national government, wouldn't this set us up for another war system when states disagreed? The use of military force against a state would be seen as a declaration of war—not as pressure to stop violating an agreement.

> It was felt by the Statesmen who framed the Constitution, and by the people who adopted it, that it was necessary that many of the rights of sovereignty which the States then possessed should be ceded to the General Government . . . .
>
> Roger B. Taney, Chief Justice
> U.S. Supreme Court

It would probably be considered by the attacked nation-state as a release from all previous contracts by which it might be bound.

John Fiske clarifies for us the problem of dealing with a nation-state when it breaks the law: "When an individual defies the law, you can lock him up in jail, or levy an execution upon his property. The immense force of the community is arrayed against him, and he is as helpless as a straw on the billows of the ocean. He cannot raise a militia to protect himself. But when the law is defied by a state, it is quite otherwise. You cannot put a state into jail, nor seize its goods; you can only make war on it, and if you try that expedient you find that the state is not helpless. Its local pride and prejudices are aroused against you, and its militia will turn out in full force to uphold the infraction of law."

How can a national government actually support state governments, protect the power of states to make their own decisions about matters within their own state borders, maintain an overall national power with the ability to enforce laws for the good of all the nation-states, and at the same time make everything as responsive as possible to the will of the people? How can you set up an overall government that adds to the *prosperity and protection* of the individual rights of everyone?

Difficult Issues

When George Washington lowered the gavel on May 25, 1787 at the first session of the Constitutional Convention, many doubted that it could be done because of the fixed instructions the states had given their delegates. For example, the Delaware delegates were prohibited from agreeing to any change in the equal vote of all the states, which they enjoyed in the Continental Congress.

The delegates soon realized that the solution to America's problems could not be achieved by revising the Articles. Something more fundamental was needed; a mere patching up would not do the job. It was up to the political geniuses assembled in Philadelphia *to put in place a new system of government* that could steer the ship of state between the shoals of ineffectiveness and the reefs of power. Delegate Randolph advised, "When the salvation of the republic is at stake, it would be treason to our trust not to propose what we find necessary."

George Washington knew that the delegates must go beyond their instructions from the states and think afresh to find the answers that would save their dream of a United States. "It is too probable that no plan we propose will be adopted," he told some delegates. "Perhaps another dreadful conflict is to be sustained. If to please the people, we offer what we ourselves disapprove, how can we afterwards defend our work?

Let us raise a standard to which the wise and honest can repair. The event is in the hand of God."

There was disagreement on almost every issue. It took patience and an ability to listen to each other to understand opposing views. The delegates were careful to control their emotions and postponed decisions on touchy issues that would blow the convention apart. They worked day by day, living with disagreement. They were determined to achieve a unified government. *The Great Rehearsal* by Carl Van Doren spells out the fascinating interplay of interests that the Constitutional delegates had to deal with. Van Doren regards the convention as a "great rehearsal" of the process that we need today to create a final layer of world governance that will give humanity a future on this planet.

The Convention almost collapsed

> . . . I have had no wish more ardent, through the whole progress of this business, than that of knowing what kind of government is best calculated for us to live under. No doubt there will be a diversity of sentiments on this important subject; and to inform the judgment, it is necessary to hear all arguments that can be advanced. To please all is impossible and to attempt it would be vain. The only way, therefore . . . is, under all the views in which it can be placed, and with due consideration to circumstances, habits, &c., &c., to form such a government as will bear the scrutinizing eye of criticism, and trust it to the good sense and patriotism of the people to carry it into effect. Demagogues, men who are unwilling to lose any of their State consequence, and interested characters in each, will oppose any general government. But let these be regarded rightly, and justice, it is to be hoped, will at length prevail.
>
> George Washington
> July 1, 1787

over the demand of small states to have an equal voice in Congress, and the demand of large states that population be proportionally represented. New York had over 300,000 residents while Delaware had fewer than 60,000. And Delaware wasn't about to be outvoted!

The solution seems so obvious now with hindsight, but then it seemed insurmountable. After all, how could you empower both the large states and the small states simultaneously—and still have an effective government? Roger Sherman of Connecticut came to the rescue; he suggested that there be two houses of Congress.

> *The Federal Convention, viewed from the records, is startlingly fresh and new. The spirit behind it was the spirit of compromise, seemingly no very noble flag to rally round. Compromise can be an ugly word, signifying a pact with the devil, a chipping off of the best to suit the worst. Yet in the Constitutional Convention the spirit of compromise reigned in grace and glory; as Washington presided, it sat on his shoulder like the dove. Men rise to speak and one sees them struggle with the bias of birthright, locality, statehood—South against North, East against West, merchant against planter. One sees them change their minds, fight against pride, and when the moment comes, admit their error.*
> **Catherine Drinker Bowen**
> *Miracle at Philadelphia*

It was eventually decided that the number of Representatives in the House was to be proportional to each state's population, and the Senate was to have two Senators from each state regardless of size—which makes all states equal. The "impossible" had been accomplished by *creative insight and compromise.*

Compromise Leads to Success

The delegates were unshakably divided over the issue of slavery and the slave trade from Africa. On August 22 George Mason of Virginia stood up and condemned "the infernal traffic." He later said, "The augmentation of slaves weakens the states; and such a trade is diabolical in itself, and disgraceful to mankind. Yet, by this constitution, it is continued. . . . As much as I value an union of all the states, I would not admit the Southern states [South Carolina and Georgia] into the union, unless they agree to the discontinuance of this disgraceful trade . . . ." George Washington, Benjamin Franklin, and most delegates from the Northern states agreed with him.

Charles Pinckney answered for the other side, "South Carolina can never receive the plan if it prohibits the slave trade." He pointed out that slavery was "justified by the example of all the world." He cited Greece, Rome, and other ancient states; he declared with finality and vehemence that South Carolina and Georgia could not do without slaves.

> The Constitution that is submitted is not free from imperfections. But there are as few radical defects in it as could well be expected, considering the heterogeneous mass of which the Convention was composed and the diversity of interests that are to be attended to. As a Constitutional door is opened for future amendments and alterations, I think it would be wise in the people to accept what is offered to them.
>
> George Washington
> On signing the U.S. Constitution

This was a rock-hard, insoluble issue that threatened to destroy the acceptance of the U.S. Constitution by the thirteen nation-states. Should they break up the U.S. into two or even three different confederations? Or in the interests of achieving the strength of a common union, should they permit this evil of the slave trade?

Rather than see their dream of a United States of America condemned to failure because of this or any other issue, the delegates chose to work out *the best agreements possible*—and leave some problems to be resolved at a later time. As expressed by John Fiske, they decided that we would have a "single powerful and pacific federal union instead of being parcelled out among forty or fifty small communities, wasting their strength and lowering their moral tone by perpetual warfare. . . . There can be little doubt that slavery and every other remnant of barbarism in American society would have thriven far more lustily under a state of chronic anarchy than was possible under the Constitution."

The issue of slavery was decided over a half-century later during President Lincoln's administration by an unfortunate civil war between the Southern and Northern states. Yet it is likely that without the compromise that let our U.S. federal government be formed, *the bloodshed over this issue and many other issues* between thirteen proud, assertive nation-states would have brought about enormously more suffering and death over the years *for both blacks and whites.* The founders of our nation *did not want to lose all* by holding out for everything they individually wanted.

> *The intolerable anarchy which was swiftly created by the exercise of autonomous sovereignty by the thirteen states over matters of common concern drove our forefathers into union. Most of them took every step in that direction with misgivings, with reluctance, and often with repugnance.*
> Vernon Nash
> *The World Must Be Governed*

It is easy to tighten one's position so that it becomes absolutely nonnegotiable—and it can feel good to pound the table with indignation and righteousness. When we do this, our ability to work together for our mutual good can be destroyed. Many people feel today that no issue should be permitted to stand in the way of creating a worldwide federation that can save humanity from "the scourge of war" and environmental ruin. Once we achieve such a world governance, we will have a fine vehicle for protecting human rights without bloodying up the planet. And freed from wasting a trillion dollars a year on global killing machines, we'll have the money to stop fouling our planetary nest.

Finishing the Job

So day after day through the long hot summer, the delegates continued their difficult work, trying to find the wavering line between too much and too little. They worked out agreements on how to enact taxes, appropriate money, and approve foreign treaties. They limited the power of all three branches of the overall government by ingenious checks and balances. Since there was no chief executive under the Articles of Confederation, they carefully laid out the limited

> *The Constitution which we now present is the result of a spirit of amity and of the mutual deference and concession which the peculiarity of our political situation rendered indispensable.*
> George Washington
> On submitting the Constitution
> to the Continental Congress

powers of the President. The functions of the Senate, House of Representatives, and Supreme Court were likewise specified. The Constitution was to go into effect when nine states ratified it. These and other details of this superb political invention were finally summed up in seven articles.

The finished product was not thoroughly satisfying to anyone at the convention. Benjamin Franklin, who was internationally viewed as one of the wisest philosophers and greatest scientists of the age, expressed the attitude of most of the delegates to the Constitutional Convention: "I confess that there are several parts of this constitution which I do not at present approve. . . ." Franklin was a master at helping people go from conflict to unity:

53

. . . But I am not sure I shall never approve them. For having lived long, I have experienced many instances of being obliged by better information or fuller consideration, to change opinions even on important subjects, which I once thought right, but found to be otherwise. It is therefore that the older I grow, the more apt I am to doubt my own judgment, and to pay more respect to the judgment of others. Most men indeed as well as most sects in religion, think themselves in possession of all truth, and that wherever others differ from them it is so far error. . . . But though many private persons think almost as highly of their own infallibility as that of their sect, few express it so naturally as a certain French lady, who in a dispute with her sister, said, "I don't know how it happens, Sister, but I meet with nobody but myself, that's always in the right"—*Il n'y a que moi qui a toujours raison.* In these sentiments, Sir, I agree to this Constitution with all its faults, if they are such. . . .

Franklin eloquently summed it up, "I consent, Sir, to this Constitution, because I expect no better and because I am not sure that it is not the best. The opinions I have had of its errors, I sacrifice to the public good. . . ."

The hesitation of our politicians today to lead us by supporting a binding world system of law and order is understandable. Carl Van Doren tells us, "Not one of the delegates about to sign could feel certain that their plan would be accepted by the state conventions or ever go into effect. They might have wasted all their time and effort. They might by their proposals have raised up political enmities which would put an end to their own public careers. They could not foresee that to have signed the Constitution would in the future make them all remembered, however little else they might have done—as the Founding Fathers of their country."

On that great Monday, September 17, 1787, the Constitution of the United States of America was signed by every state delegation present. Of those present, only Governor Randolph and Colonel Mason from Virginia, and Elbridge Gerry from Massachusetts individually refused to sign. It is warming to note that Gerry would later become a representative to the first Congress of the new nation and Vice President under Madison, and that Randolph would be the Attorney General and Secretary of State under Washington.

Approval by the People

The Philadelphia convention sent its proposed constitution to the Continental Congress in New York, which sent it to the state legislatures. The state legislatures called for state conventions that would decide if the people were in favor of this new vehicle for governing themselves.

Patrick Henry didn't like it. (You'll recall he roused people in the spirit of '76 with his famous "Give me liberty or give me death.") He predicted that a state-established religion would be set up under the new Constitution, and Kentuckians would lose the right to navigate the Mississippi River. Mason attacked the character of the Constitutional delegates, calling them "Knaves and Fools," "a parcel of Coxcombs," and "Office Hunters not a few."

> *Whilst the last members were signing it, Doctr. Franklin looking towards the Presidents chair, at the back of which a rising sun happened to be painted, observed to a few members near him, that Painters had found it difficult to distinguish in their art a rising from a setting sun. I have, said he, . . . often in the course of the Session, and the vicissitudes of my hopes and fears as to its issue, looked at that behind the President without being able to tell whether it was rising or setting: But now at length I have the happiness to know that it is a rising and not a setting Sun.*
> James Madison, Delegate
> Constitutional Convention
> September 1787

George Washington in a letter to Lafayette on February 7, 1788 said, "It appears to me, then, little short of a miracle, that the Delegates from so many different states (which states you know are also different from each other), in their manners, circumstances, and prejudices, should unite in forming a system of national government. . . ." Supporters for the new federal constitution had an uphill battle. One future president, Monroe, and the fathers of two future presidents, Harrison and Tyler, were anti-federalists who fought against ratification.

> It may be just a matter of time before the concepts of our Founding Fathers are extended to the entire human race. True, many think this is a dream, but the real dreamers may be those who expect that their children will make it, given on the one hand an arms race virtually out of control, expanding political terrorism, global pollution and nuclear proliferation, and on the other hand the rickety and inadequate global structures to contain these threats to human survival.
>
> Eric Cox, Field Director
> World Federalist Association

The signers of the Constitution did not abandon their baby, but worked diligently at the state level to secure ratification. Hamilton and Madison (with some help from John Jay) published a series of 85 essays entitled *The Federalist*. All were signed "Publius." These were picked up by the newspapers, and the issues were strenuously debated by the people as the big controversy of the day.

While working for ratification, Hamilton responded to the accusation that he was too cynical when he said that the solemn pledges of nations are untrustworthy. Hamilton retorted, "Do we depend for the maintenance of domestic order upon the mere promises of individuals to behave themselves?" Then he profoundly posed:

Why has government been instituted at all? Because the passions of men will not conform to the dictates of reason and justice without restraint. Has it been found that bodies of men act with more rectitude and greater disinterestedness than individuals? The contrary of this has been inferred by all accurate observers of the conduct of mankind.

Before meeting in Philadelphia, Delaware had instructed its delegates not to have anything to do with a constitution that did not give it an equal vote with all other states. On December 7, 1787, Delaware was the first to ratify—quickly and without a single dissenting vote! When the Pennsylvania state convention was meeting to consider ratification, it received the news that Delaware had ratified. One of the delegates, Smilie, sourly commented that Delaware had "reaped the honor of

> The moment this plan goes forth, all other considerations will be laid aside—and the greatest question will be, shall there be a national government or not? And this must take place or a general anarchy will be the alternative.
>
> Gouverneur Morris, Delegatge
> Constitutional Convention, 1787

having first surrendered the liberties of the people." The majority of the delegates, however, felt that Pennsylvania's liberty and future prosperity would be better protected by being part of the federal union. They voted to ratify the constitution only four days after Delaware ratified!

This was followed by New Jersey, Georgia, Connecticut, Massachusetts, Maryland, and South Carolina. On June 21, 1788, New Hampshire was the ninth state to ratify, and thereby completed the number needed for the new federal government to go into effect. Just four days later Virginia ratified by a 10-vote majority and New York by only 3 votes. On August 2, 1788, North Carolina declined to act on the new constitution but changed its mind a year and a half later. It joined the Union on November 21, 1789.

Rhode Island had been torn in a conflict between the townspeople and farmers. It had not even sent delegates to the Constitutional Convention in 1787. After the federal government had been in operation for two years, the Senate told the state that it was severing commercial relations between the United States and Rhode Island. Its ships would have to go through customs and immigration just like foreign vessels from England and France.

> There were times in the Convention of 1787 when it seemed that the requirements of the individual states in their nationalistic American world were insurmountable. But the American Constitution has proved that none of the American "nations" actually had interests that were more vital to them than were the interests of America as a whole.
> Lloyd Graham
> The Desperate People

Rhode Island finally realized that it could not provide itself with the security and prosperity that would be possible for its citizens if it joined the federal union. By a margin of only two votes, three years after the Constitutional Convention, Rhode Island ratified the Constitution of the United States on May 29, 1790. Now all thirteen of the original nation-states had come together in creating *a federal government that permitted the greatness of all the individual states to unfold!* At the urging of the citizens of various states, the first ten amendments to the U.S. Constitution (the Bill of Rights) were quickly ratified.

Our Way Is Clear

"In 1787," Carl Van Doren explains in *The Great Rehearsal,* "the problem was how the people could learn to think nationally, not locally, about the United States." The problem today is how the people can learn to *think internationally, not nationally, about the world.* Surely, there will be opposition to the idea. Some may call it naive, idealistic, or premature. These were the same attitudes that our Founding Fathers overcame—and so can we.

There are some who argue that creating a world congress, courts, and an executive branch is much more difficult today than it was in the simpler world of our forefathers two hundred years ago. That may be true, but we should not forget that our technical means of communication and the ability to solve complex problems is now infinitely greater. The compelling urgency of the need should provide the extra inspiration and determination to overcome the obstacles.

The challenges that faced America back then must have seemed as great to them as ours do to us. Patriot Tom Paine noted that the thirteen colonies were "made up of people from different nations, accustomed to different forms and habits of government, speaking different languages, and more different in their models of worship." Pennsylvania and Delaware had religious freedom for Christians; in Rhode Island Catholics could not vote; and in Massachusetts, Catholic priests were liable to imprisonment for life! They had no common currency or system of taxation, and there were trade and travel restrictions between the states. They

> *The federal idea, which our Founding Fathers applied in their historical act of political creation in the eighteenth century, can be applied in this twentieth century in the larger context of the world of free nations—if we will but match our forefathers in courage and vision.*
>
> Nelson A. Rockefeller
> *The Future of Federalism*
> Harvard University Press

were divided into liberals and conservatives. Some depended upon slavery for their existence, and others regarded it as an abomination. It was North vs. South, East vs. West, planter vs. merchant, and one religion against another. Some of the states were talking about war with each other!

Yet with all this diversity, two centuries ago the patriots put the Constitution together in about 100 working days (May 25 to September 17). From conception on September 17, 1787 to official birth on June 21, 1788, our federal republic only took nine months! And in those days it took three weeks to travel from Philadelphia to Atlanta! And no telephones or fax machines either!

> *There is one thing stronger than all the armies of the world and that is an idea whose time has come.*
> Victor Hugo

The Federal Solution

The Founding Fathers accomplished this great union by designing a government that *honored and included* the thirteen separate nation-states instead of putting itself in opposition to them as unruly delinquents to be punished when they got out of line. They did this by leaving each nation-state in control of almost all the decisions that affect its own citizens. Since the people of each state had their own state legislatures, it was up to the voters to make sure they were getting the state government they wanted. Then they minimized the risk of interstate conflict by creating an added layer of federal government that would handle national problems that could not be solved by individual states. The national government could make and enforce decisions that required states to cooperate with each other and to support activities that served the common good.

This political invention has been tested by the U.S. for over 200 years—and it has been copied by dozens of other nations throughout the world.

We must learn how to become planetary patriots. We can apply the federal solution to create a world congress, a world court, and world enforcement. Our families will no longer be threatened by a Wild West world of anarchy.

To Sum Up

In our own way, we must *adapt* this basic political invention to the world of today. To do this you will need to take Step 4 (explained in the next chapter), in which we recognize the enormous progress we've made in the last forty years toward world law, courts, and enforcement. We can be optimistic about achieving our ultimate right to live with dignity in a peaceful world free from the threat of death by war. We're not starting at the bottom of the ladder—in fact we're nearly at the top!!!

> The real cause of all wars has always been the same . . . . Wars between groups of men forming social units always take place when these units—tribes, dynasties, churches, cities, nations— exercise unrestricted sovereign power. Wars between these social units cease the moment sovereign power is transferred from them to a larger or higher unit . . . . The question is not one of 'surrendering' national sovereignty. The problem is not negative and does not involve giving up something we already have. The problem is positive—creating something we lack . . . but imperatively need . . . the extension of law and order into another field of human association which heretofore has remained unregulated and in anarchy.
>
> Emery Reves
> *The Anatomy of Peace*

We expect that you will be amazed by our progress so far—and deeply inspired to help the world complete the final layer of government on which our common survival depends.

You'll recall the story of patriot Paul Revere, who galloped across the countryside to warn people of the approach of the English troops: "The Redcoats are coming!" Will you appoint yourself a 21st Century Paul Revere? Will you make sure that your neighbors are awakening to the greatest dangers humanity has ever faced? And will you tell them the great news of how we can reform the United Nations (explained in Step 5) and take the other necessary steps to save ourselves and our children—and give all people of this planet more security and a richer life than ever before?

As modern Paul Reveres, let's not stop until the job is done.

4th Step

*Recognize
Our Great
Progress*

More progress has been made in *international law* in the past forty years than in previous thousands. We must escape from being discouraged by judgments of "too idealistic," "utopian," or "not practical." If we peer into the past, we will better appreciate the present. In the evolution of law, courts, and enforcement—the essential building blocks for a peaceful world—the perspective of history reveals *an almost incredible record of recent accomplishment.*

The world has been getting ready for a great transformation! In fact, it has already begun with the dramatic events among Eastern European nations beginning in 1989. On November 3, 1989 the United States and the Soviet Union sponsored a U.N. resolution for

> *... the salvation of this human world lies nowhere else than in the human heart, in the human power to reflect, in human meekness and in human responsibility.*
> Vaclav Havel
> President of Czechoslovakia
> At Joint Meeting U.S. Congress

enhancing international peace and security. They jointly declared that this resolution represented "a new spirit of constructive cooperation."

The Growth of International Law

It took thousands of years to move from the primitive law of the pre-Christian era to the beginnings of international law. We are indebted to the swashbuckling pirates for the first clear beginnings of international criminal law. As they plundered ships on the high seas, they obviously were not subject to the territorial laws of any one country. Since they threatened the free flow of commerce, something had to be done. By common understanding of maritime nations, they were outlawed as "the enemies of all mankind" and tried and punished wherever and whenever they might be captured. *Separate nations were able to cooperate to solve a common problem.* Because of this, piracy is no longer a serious concern.

> *It is obvious that no difficulty in the way of a world government can match the danger of a world without it.*
>
> Carl Van Doren
> *The Great Rehearsal*

One of the early founders of international law was Franciscus de Victoria, a Spaniard who studied at the Sorbonne in Paris before being appointed Primary Professor of Sacred Theology at the University of Salamanca in 1526. He taught that all wars have to be morally justifiable—to right a wrong.

According to Victoria, the personal glory of a king or differences of religion were not acceptable reasons for killing people of other nations. He said that no subject was bound to serve in an unjust war even if commanded by his king. This bad news for the tyrants could only be published 150 years after Victoria's death. It was assembled from his students' lecture notes. Victoria is recognized as one of the pioneers of international law. His statue stands in the garden outside the United Nations today.

The person universally acclaimed as the father of international law is the great Dutch jurist Hugo Grotius. In 1625 he completed his famous three books entitled *Laws of War and Peace*. Grotius listed three methods to prevent violence between nations: (1) conferences,

(2) arbitration, or (3) by lot, as had been suggested by Solomon. He explained that as a much lesser evil than a killing war between armies, the kings and tyrants might settle their differences by single combat between themselves—an idea that the U.N. seems to have overlooked! He urged that we have humane conduct even in war, ". . . lest by imitating wild beasts too much we forget to be human."

The first chair for the teaching of "the law of nations" was established at the University of Heidelberg, and Samuel Pufendorf was its first professor. He published *On the Law of Nature and Nations* in 1688. Even at the time of the Constitutional Convention in Philadelphia, the expression "international law" was still virtually unknown. This term had been introduced only several years earlier by Jeremy Bentham when he published *Principles of International Law* in 1783.

> But the national sovereign state in its present form is an anachronism, chained to its tribal preoccupations and ambitions, incapable of transcending the national interest in favor of the human interest.
>
> Norman Cousins, President
> World Federalist Association
> Author, *Anatomy of an Illness*

David Dudley Field was among the notables who contributed to a flood of ideas in international law. He had codified the laws of the state of New York and was the first president of the unofficial International Law Association. In 1872 he drafted *Outlines of an International Code,* which called for arbitration of disputes and collective enforcement actions. Professor Pasquale Fiore of Italy in 1880 for the first time referred to the "scourge of war" as the "greatest of all crimes." *The seeds of international law were sprouting and taking root.*

In the 20th Century

In an attempt to relieve the very heavy burden of the arms race, Nicholas II, the Czar of Russia, proposed in 1899 that the "civilized states" meet at The Hague for what was heralded as the first "international peace conference." It was attended by 26 nations. In the second Hague conference, in 1907, the number of participants increased to 44—a measure of progress. Unfortunately, they largely dealt with international rules for military combat, as they were unwilling to genuinely give up their age-old privilege of settling disputes by killing people in other nations. Instead of laying down binding rules for peace, all that the self-styled "civilized states" could do was to agree upon rules for waging war!

It took World War I, with 10 million people killed, for nations to realize that the prevailing international system was in need of revision. All people everywhere yearned for a more secure and peaceful world. President Woodrow Wilson played a leading role in establishing the League of Nations as "a general association of nations" to protect "great and small states alike." *The 1919 Covenant for a League of Nations, based upon ideas that had been evolving for centuries, envisaged codification of international law, a court to settle disputes, arms control, collective security, and social justice.*

> *There can be no peace without law.*
> Dwight D. Eisenhower
> U.S. President
> October 31, 1956

It was a great milestone in the zig-zagging line of progress toward a world government. But a handful of isolationist Senators headed by Henry Cabot Lodge blocked American membership in the League of Nations. The nation that had conceived the infant abandoned its own child. The U.S. never joined. *It was not the League that failed the nations; the nations failed the League.* Thus the door was opened to the even greater tragedy of World War II with 35 million killed.

A Giant Step Forward

After World War II, international law took a great leap ahead. In 1945, the United States again took the lead in proposing an improved system of international law and order. The goal expressed in the Charter of the United Nations was "to maintain international peace and security . . . in conformity with the principles of justice and international law."

> *What has resulted [the U.N. Charter] is a human document with human imperfections but with human hopes and human victory as well. But whatever its imperfections, the Charter . . . offers the world an instrument by which a real beginning may be made upon the work of peace.*
>
> Report of the U.S. Secretary of State to the President, 1945

With a new fervor, special U.N. committees were assigned to codify laws among nations. Within the next few decades, aggression, genocide, and crimes against humanity were unanimously condemned as criminal acts. Declarations spelled out the civil, political, economic, social, and cultural rights of all peoples. International accords opened the door to freedom from colonialism.

Inspired by the U.N., nations agreed on "Principles of International Law Governing Friendly Relations Among States." Apartheid was declared an international crime. Aggression was defined by consensus. The Helsinki Agreement sought to ensure "Security and

Cooperation in Europe." Conventions outlawed torture, the taking of hostages, and other acts of terrorism. Work was begun on a comprehensive code of offenses against the peace and security of mankind. The monumental Law of the Sea was accepted by many nations. Multinational treaties were signed in great profusion.

Admittedly, key provisions were often left deliberately vague and open to conflicting interpretations. But that should come as no surprise. *Nations were just beginning to learn that the sovereignty of the state must yield to the sovereignty of the law.* The U.N. Charter was another important step forward, but we were not there yet. It was deliberately put together with nonbinding loopholes that made it unable to preserve peace. Since 1945 there have been about 130 wars, with an estimated 16 million dead. The antiquated veto system kept the Security Council from using its Charter-given power to stop the killing.

International Courts Begin

We've now looked at the first great steps in which humankind attempted to create lasting peace through international global cooperation: the League of Nations and the United Nations. Now let's examine the great progress we've made in this century in the evolution of international courts. Just as the growth of law from earliest times was a slow and difficult *but continually accelerating* process, history reveals a similar evolutionary pattern regarding the courts needed to settle disputes by peaceful means.

The Hague meetings at the turn of the century recognized the need for a system to settle disputes peacefully, but all they could agree upon at that time was a weak procedure for arbitration.

On the American continent, a Central American Court of Justice was created in 1908 as part of a peace treaty signed by several Central American republics. The national legislators of five participating states elected the five judges. Each nation let go of some of its sovereignty when it agreed to be bound by the decision of the Court. The agreements creating this Court were scheduled to expire in ten years. Between 1908 and 1918, ten cases came before it. One of its decrees (involving a complaint by Honduras) that Guatemala and El Salvador were supporting a revolution against Honduras may have prevented a new Central American war. *Despite its limited period of life, the Central American Court of Justice was the first international tribunal of its kind in history.*

> *World federation is an idea that will not die. More and more people are coming to realize that peace must be more than an interlude if we are to survive; that peace is a product of law and order; that law is essential if the force of arms is not to rule the world.*
>
> William O. Douglas
> Former Justice
> U.S. Supreme Court

Following World War I, the stronger Permanent Court of International Justice was established at The Hague. But nations were not yet ready to accept the recommendations of legal experts. The new institution, commonly known as the World Court, was only authorized to settle disputes "which the parties thereto shall submit to it." Would you feel safe if an alleged murderer in your town could be tried by a court only if he or she agreed to it?

Even with this serious shortcoming, the Permanent Court was an improvement over what had existed before. In the brief period between world wars, its opinions helped to clarify and develop international law. After 1945, it was renamed The International Court of Justice, its procedures were improved, and its work now continues under the U.N. Charter. It is staffed by fifteen outstanding judges from various nations.

> One should not forget the capacities of the International Court.... The General Assembly and the Security Council could approach it more often for consultative conclusions on international disputes. Its mandatory jurisdiction should be recognized by all on mutually agreed upon conditions.
>
> Mikhail Gorbachev
> Soviet General Secretary
> Article in *Pravda*,
> September 17, 1987

After World War II—*for the first time*—temporary international criminal tribunals were established at Nuremberg, Tokyo, and elsewhere to try German and Japanese war criminals for crimes against peace, war crimes, and crimes against humanity. This established a legal precedent for trying international criminals such as Hitler, Hussein, and Pol Pot. The safety of citizens of this planet requires laws, courts, and enforcement directly charging *individuals* who commit crimes against humanity. Individuals, *not nations*, are the criminals—and must be held accountable.

Permanent International Courts

Many permanent multinational courts have been established. The best example is the Court of Justice of the European Community. This Court has compulsory jurisdiction to settle disputes that arise under treaties that established the Common Market and the European Atomic Energy Community. *It has settled thousands of commercial disputes, which in the past frequently led to military conflicts.* Now a dozen

European nations use international law instead of armies to settle such disagreements!

The European Court of Human Rights at Strasbourg protects individual rights in Western Europe. "Most citizens of the member states of the Council of Europe (21 at present)," according to Ferdinand Kinksy, "have their human rights not only guaranteed by their own national constitution, but also by the European convention for human rights. Should their national government violate their human rights, European citizens have the possibility to go to a European court, whose judgment has to be respected by the individual states. The member states of the European communities (the twelve Common Market countries) did transfer part of their sovereignty to the community's institutions. Of course, these 'pre-federalist' elements are not sufficient to make a true federation of the European Community. Neither foreign nor security policies are covered by the EEC treaties." But a new European Parliament is beginning to deal with problems with political consequences.

> *Military spending is qualitatively different from all other domestic economic activity because its output is directed external to the society. In relationship to the domestic economy, military spending is not productive of any good or service. It consumes personal energy and resources without giving anything productive back to the economy.*
> Robert W. Reuschlein
> Author, *Peace Economics: Newest Scientific Proof That Military Spending Causes Decline*

The new Inter-American Court of Human Rights in Costa Rica is beginning to follow a pattern similar to the European court. International agencies, dealing with such areas as banking, health, labor, trade, and atomic energy, have developed legal procedures for settling disputes. New administrative tribunals of all kinds have begun to flourish. Today proposals are being considered for an international court to resolve conflicts relating to outer space and environmental problems.

The Law of the Sea Treaty requires almost all disputes to be settled by an international tribunal. It is in the process of being ratified by various nations. Unfortunately the U.S. has not yet ratified it. The proposed International Criminal Court to deal with international terrorism was endorsed by the American Bar Association in 1978. As a neutral forum, it could avoid today's problems in extraditing terrorists who take advantage of national boundary lines to escape justice.

> We must establish a rule of law, a world rule of law. We have to realize that the world needs policemen who serve the interests of all mankind.
> Ramsey Clark
> Former U.S. Attorney General

The Soviet Union is also moving toward the position taken by the American Bar Association. In an article published on September 17, 1987, General Secretary Gorbachev wrote: "A drastic intensification and expansion of cooperation between states in uprooting international terrorism is extremely important. It would be expedient to concentrate this cooperation within the framework of the United Nations organization. In our opinion, it would be useful to create under its aegis a tribunal to investigate acts of international terrorism. . . ."

In 1989, legislation was pending in Congress to create an international criminal court to combat terrorism. The United Nations voted on December 4, 1989 to consider such a court to deal with drug traffickers. It is now being studied by the International Law Commission. Contrary to its long tradition, the Soviet Union seemed disposed to go along with such tribunals. It also agreed with the United States to accept the compulsory jurisdiction of the International Court of Justice in interpreting a number of human rights treaties.

Despite the hesitation of some important countries, the record shows that nations are gradually becoming accustomed to letting go of enough sovereignty to settle disputes in international courts instead of on the battlefield. War and killing are damaging and expensive; doing combat in international courts is a real bargain by comparison! Humanity can no longer afford to pay the price of the costly method of going to war.

Regional Cooperation Increases

Regional thinking and organization have today become a fact of life all over the globe. As we mentioned in the Second Step, despite centuries of feuds, linguistic differences, and cultural barriers, the West European states have formed a European Community and elected a European Parliament. These rival countries, which had suffered the horrible ravages of centuries of war, were determined to begin trading, working, and living together in peaceful community.

> The international community should support a system of laws to regularize international relations and maintain the peace in the same manner that law governs national order.
> Pope John Paul II

As smaller nations have come to recognize their need for more security, they have increasingly joined in new cooperative associations and coalitions to enhance their economic, religious, political, or other interests. The Organization of American States has been formed. The Organization of African Unity has come into existence. The League of Arab States has been created. Nordic states have joined together for expanded coalition. Southeast Asian Nations have formed a similar coalition for the Pacific. Developing countries have formed the "Group of 77." Over a hundred nations have belied their "nonaligned" status by aligning themselves to further their common interests.

> *The only security for Americans today, or for any people, is in the creation of a system of world order that enables nations to retain sovereignty over their own cultures and institutions but that creates a workable authority for regulating the behavior of nations in their relationships with one another.*
>
> Norman Cousins, President
> World Federalist Association

A host of international organizations and specialized agencies, both governmental and nongovernmental, have taken steps toward planethood in hundreds of ways that were inconceivable not long ago. The better known organizations include the International Atomic Energy Agency, the International Maritime Organization, the International Civil Aviation Organization, and the World Meteorological Organization. Many other agencies dealing with health, commerce, finance, trade, and development are now operating. *Within recent memory, the land, the seas, and the skies have become areas of increasing international cooperation.*

This does not mean that they've yet achieved full planethood within their regions. But it does mean the world is gradually exploring the benefits of going beyond anarchy to get the enormous benefits of solidly lawful cooperation.

Enforcing International Law

Now let's turn our attention to the steps we've taken toward enforcing international law. Here we'll also find an emerging pattern of gradual progress. The Covenant of the League of Nations and the U.N. Charter both provided for enforcement by economic sanctions, control of armaments, and an international army—but the plans have never been put into effect because the major powers have failed to live up to their obligations.

However, in 1950 in Korea, an international military force under U.N. command was sent into action to halt aggression. This was "the first effort to enforce the principles of collective security through a worldwide international organization." When war erupted in the Congo in 1960, a U.N. military force was authorized to restore law and order and to expel foreign troops from the newly independent country. For over 20 years, U.N. peacekeeping forces have been deployed in Cyprus to prevent war between Turkish and Greek nationalists.

In the Middle East, when Egypt nationalized the Suez Canal in 1956, Israel, France, and England invaded the country to protect their interests. The Security Council was powerless because of the British and French veto. But the Soviet Union and the United States arranged for an Emergency Session of the General

> *If the rule of law is to govern the community of states and protect it against violations of the international public order, it can only be satisfactorily established by the promulgation of an international penal code and by the permanent functioning of an international criminal jurisdiction.*
>
> Richard Alfaro, 1950
> Former President of Panama

Assembly. *Even though it had no Charter authority, the Assembly voted to establish an international force to halt the hostilities.* A U.N. Emergency Force from ten nations was quickly assembled. The invaders cleared out in a hurry!

In 1967, a unanimous decision of the Security Council demanded a cease-fire and ended the fighting between Egypt and Israel within six days. In 1973, an agreement between U.S. Secretary of State Kissinger and Soviet Chairman Brezhnev brought the "Day of Atonement" war to an abrupt halt. When the superpowers were united, peace became enforceable. In the Introduction we noted the speed with which the Security Council acted in August 1990 when Iraq invaded Kuwait.

> *Needed changes will only come about as the expression of the political will of peoples in many parts of the world.*
>
> Olaf Palme, 1982
> Former Prime Minister of Sweden
> Chairman, Ind. Comm. on
> Disarmament and Security

United Nations peacekeeping forces, relying more on armbands than on arms, are playing an increasingly useful role in separating antagonists and monitoring borders in many regions. They won the Nobel Peace Prize in 1988. They can do much more for peace if they are strengthened, supported, and given a fair chance.

Progress in Social Justice

International concern for human rights and welfare is a great historical force of our time. One can hardly imagine the chaos and increased suffering that would exist in the world today were it not for cooperative actions taken during the past few decades by

U.N. organizations. (See Appendix 2 for their outstanding contribution to the people of the world.)

The World Health Organization, for example, has totally eradicated smallpox from the face of the earth and all but eliminated malaria. The Food and Agriculture Organization has "freedom from hunger" as its goal. U.N. programs deal with housing, the rights of women and children, the physically handicapped, refugees, the illiterate, the uneducated,

> There is one overriding truth in this nuclear age—no nation can achieve security by itself.... Security in the nuclear age means common security. This has been the central conclusion of our commission.
>
> Cyrus Vance, 1982
> Former U.S. Secretary of State
> *Common Security:*
> *A Blueprint for Survival*

and the disadvantaged in many fields. Economic aid to underdeveloped countries has become a primary world concern.

It was Ambassador Arvid Pardo, of the tiny island of Malta, who gave expression to the inspiring dream that the vast resources of the ocean were "the common heritage of mankind." That humanitarian principle is slowly moving toward reality today. It was confirmed in a 1967 treaty governing the moon and outer space and a 1980 treaty covering the vast continent of Antarctica. Most nations are beginning to accept the idea that all of humankind should somehow share the untapped wealth of our planet.

In the short space of one lifetime—hardly a blink in the eye of time—there has been an awakening of the human conscience. Human rights are now monitored and protected by many governments and organizations around the world. *We are slowly edging in the direction of an international cooperation.*

Progress Toward Disarmament

The problem of disarmament is the heart of the most vital challenge to the international order. Both the Covenant of the League of Nations and the U.N. Charter called for reductions of national arms.

> What is called for is total disarmament—universal, enforceable and complete.
>
> John J. McCloy, 1959
> Former U.S. Asst. Sec. of War

The wisdom of the plan was recognized, even though states were not yet ready to implement it. In the intervening years, however, slow and steady progress has been made.

In 1959, Soviet Premier Nikita Khrushchev, speaking at the United Nations, called for general and complete disarmament. In 1961 President John F. Kennedy appointed John J. McCloy, a former Assistant Secretary of War and a distinguished public servant, to serve as his Special Assistant for Disarmament and to seek an agreement with the Russians.

In September of that year, McCloy and Deputy Soviet Foreign Minister Zorin drew up a joint statement of principles in which both sides recognized that general and complete disarmament was the goal of both nations. They agreed that disarmament was to take place under *"strict and effective international controls."* New institutions would be created to settle disputes by peaceful means. An international peace force would replace national armed forces, which would be disbanded. The intelligent, concise McCloy-Zorin plan was promptly hailed by the entire General Assembly of the United Nations.

President Kennedy challenged the Soviet Union not to an arms race but to a peace race "to advance together step by step, stage by stage, until general and complete disarmament has actually been achieved." The heads of state of the two superpowers publicly declared before the whole world that they both favored general and complete disarmament. Unfortunately, suspicion and fear of change continued to paralyze both nations.

Although the excellent McCloy-Zorin plan for general and complete disarmament was never implemented, *it showed how strongly many people in the U.S., in the U.S.S.R., and throughout the globe* want to secure the ultimate human right to live with dignity in a healthy environment free from the threat of war.

> *We can not help but see that the United States and other nuclear powers are testing their most destructive weapons on other peoples' land. We have a map of the world showing how all atomic and nuclear tests have been conducted on the territory of native peoples.*
>
> Western Shoshone
> National Council
> Great Basin, Nevada

The door of opportunity has now been opened. Through planethood we can enjoy peace and environmental stability. Let us create our future not by instruments of death but through an improved international system based on laws, courts, and effective enforcement.

Our Continuing Progress

Nuclear-free zones have already been created by common consent in many areas of the world, including outer space and the moon. Some limits have been placed on nuclear weapons tests. There are agreements to cope with nuclear accidents, and "hot-lines" have been introduced to reduce the risks of miscalculation.

The Anti-Ballistic Missile Treaty of 1972 (ABM), which was ratified as part of SALT I (Strategic Arms

Limitations Talks), constituted a major step forward. Restraints on nuclear proliferation have been accepted. SALT II—even though not ratified by the United States—has generally been honored by both sides.

Thirty-five nations meeting in 1986 at the Stockholm Conference on Security in Europe agreed to notify each other of military maneuvers and to allow on-site inspections. It was, according to the West German ambassador, "a victory of reason, responsibility and realism." The Forty-nation Committee on Disarmament, after 18 years of effort, announced on April 29, 1987 that a pact banning all chemical weapons was expected early in 1988. (We still don't have it, but it's expected soon.) It was announced that the U.S. and U.S.S.R. had agreed on a joint exploration of the cosmos. The Declaration on the Non-Use of Force that had been debated at the U.N. for many years was adopted by consensus at the end of 1987. It had its loopholes but was nonetheless a significant step forward.

> *I do feel that some minimum of global government to abolish war, to cope with pollution, is absolutely necessary.*
> Arnold Toynbee
> Noted Historian

Some ice was broken in Iceland when President Reagan and Soviet General Secretary Gorbachev met at Reykjavik in October 1986. The summit meeting demonstrated how close the two leaders could come to major arms accords—and how they were able to agree on common goals.

On the difficult problem of verification, former Presidents Gerald Ford and Jimmy Carter, following an unofficial conference with Soviet experts in the spring of 1985, confirmed that past agreements had basically been followed. Carter was convinced "that even the more contentious issues could be resolved by the superpowers in a mutually satisfactory way." President Reagan's Commission on Strategic Forces (which employed the services of two former National Security Advisors, four former Secretaries of Defense, three former CIA Directors, and two former Secretaries of State) concluded that the goal of an effective verification system "remains within our reach." Indeed, an effective agreement on verification *was* reached in December 1987.

> *The dogmas of the quiet past are inadequate to the stormy present. We must think anew and act anew.*
> Abraham Lincoln

The INF Treaty signed by Reagan and Gorbachev in December 1987 provides for the elimination of all intermediate-range nuclear missiles. Other nuclear arms reductions are being discussed. We hope this and other steps toward disarmament can be implemented. *However, it will be mostly window-dressing to look good to the public (and hopefully save some money) until decision makers and their supporters are willing to take a chance for peace through world law, courts, and enforcement.*

The reduction of nuclear missiles is only a beginning. **Conventional arms today are enormously more effective at killing than the equipment used in World War II.** Missiles carrying poison gas (as used in the Iraq-Iran war) compete with nuclear weapons in their ability to destroy life on this planet. Planethood requires us to remove all arms from the control of individual nations (except for police equipment needed to keep order within their own boundaries). Only then, with international peacekeeping forces, will we have the peace and security that we had hoped to achieve through armaments.

On Toward Success

Six tapestries adorn the halls of the U.N. Palace in Geneva (the original Peace Palace for the League of Nations). They tell the story of our aspirations and progress toward an improved structure of international society. The artists depict the evolution of social life from the family to the clan, the village, the feudal estate, the national state, and—finally—to an international

> *I am strongly convinced that the best method of ultimately securing disarmament is the establishment of an international court and the development of a code of international equity which nations will recognize as affording a better method of settling international controversies than war.*
>
> Howard Taft, 1910
> U.S. President

system of government in which people of all races are joined together in a circle of peace. In the course of some six thousand years of recorded history, humankind has been slowly moving toward that sublime ideal. We're almost there!

It took the American Revolution to create the chaos that led to the birth of the Federal Constitution. It took World War I with 10 million dead and 20 million wounded to inspire statesmen to bring forth a League of Nations. It took World War II with 35 million killed to induce the nation-states to create the United Nations. Each was a great step forward.

Because of the great progress we have made in developing and using international law in the 20th Century, we are now ready to take the final step toward planethood. We can be inspired by the progress we

5th Step

Make the U.N. Effective for the 21st Century

have made, step by step, decade by decade, toward international law, international courts of justice, and international enforcement.

This Fourth Step to lasting peace and prosperity through planethood suggests that we recognize our great progress. This background is essential to convincingly explain to others the practicality of our great vision for rescuing humanity.

> *Our world family of several billion individuals on one little planet in the fathomless universe and eternal stream of time, that is the central challenge of tomorrow's Earth's government.*
> Robert Muller
> Former U.N. Assistant Sec.-Gen.
> Chancellor, University for Peace
> Author, *A Planet of Hope*

The 21st Century draws near. We've been window-shopping long enough. Now it's time to buy! The next chapter, explaining the Fifth Step, tells us how to do this by updating our vehicle for stopping war and maintaining our planetary home. Victory lies before us!

Since the end of World War II, our failure to create an effective world system to govern the planet has resulted in millions killed, many more injured, businesses disrupted, lives twisted through fear and hatred, property destroyed, environmental pollution and degeneration accelerated, and money wasted on killing machines (this term includes both people and guns). The insanity of nuclear killing machines is making us realize that World War III (with possibly 5 *billion* fatalities) may bring about the end of all people on this planet. It is the plea of *PlanetHood* that we end the arms race—not the human race.

> *If we want peace, we must reform, restructure and strengthen the United Nations.*
> Dr. John Logue, Director
> Common Heritage Institute, 1985

The First Four Steps

Let's briefly review the steps we've covered so far. Step One requires us to assert our ultimate human right to live with dignity in a healthy environment free from the threat of war. Step Two asks us to understand the new top layer of government we need in order to nail down this ultimate human right for you and your family for all time—no more international anarchy. We need to complete the governmental structure of the world with a limiting constitution setting up *a lawmaking body* (representing the people of the world), *a world court* (staffed with the wisest judges chosen from among the nations of the world), and *an effective system of sanctions and peacekeeping forces* to enforce the agreed standards of national behavior. This final layer of government would globally ensure our basic human rights, protect the sovereignty of nations, settle disputes legally, and protect the environment.

By taking Step Three we realize what it means to become a Planethood Patriot. We are urged to step into George Washington's footsteps in creating and supporting a new constitution to govern the nations of the world. The Federal Republic of the World must be strong enough to avoid ineffectiveness, and have checks and balances to limit power and avoid tyranny. This is secured by a *wise balance of power* between the legislative, executive, and judicial branches.

> *When we get to the point, as one day we will, that both sides know that in any outbreak of general hostilities, regardless of the element of surprise, destruction will be both reciprocal and complete, possibly we will have sense enough to meet at the conference table with the understanding that the era of armaments has ended and the human race must conform its actions to this truth or die.*
>
> Dwight D. Eisenhower
> U.S. President
> Personal letter, April 4, 1965

In Step Four we acknowledge our enormous progress over the past century in creating international law. We have been gradually globalizing. We note how the nations of the world have been getting accustomed to working with each other—*gradually and safely* yielding small portions of their sovereignty in order to benefit from binding international agreements for the common good. We see that nation-states are already merging into larger economic and political entities to meet their common needs—such as the European union. *There is a growing awareness that the world system must change to meet the challenge of the 21st Century.*

In Step Five we will discuss updating our vehicle for survival—the U.N.—as we move toward an effective world system with checks and balances to protect our rights and freedoms. This step is primarily concerned with spelling out how we need to reform the U.N. to ensure world peace.

After the carnage of World War II with 35 million dead, many nations were determined not to go through that again. Toward the end of the war we began to plan the United Nations Organization. In October 1945 the Charter was ratified by 50 nations at San Francisco. Enthusiasm ran high. "The U.N.

> *When there is a problem between two small nations, the problem disappears. When there is a problem between a big country and a small country, the little country disappears. When there is a problem between two big countries, the United Nations disappears.*
>
> Victor Belaunde
> Peruvian U.N. Ambassador

Charter can be a greater Magna Carta," said John Foster Dulles, our Secretary of State, who was a delegate to the San Francisco conference.

It's interesting to note that the U.N. Charter was completed on June 26, 1945—six weeks before Hiroshima and Nagasaki. This may help explain its weakness. The delegates were unaware of the devastation we would face in the nuclear era. They did not know that humanity's survival would be at stake. They failed to understand that we could no longer drag our feet in replacing international anarchy with enforced international law.

The Security Council

The Charter provides for a Security Council and a General Assembly. The Security Council was supposed to be the enforcement arm. Its five permanent members were victorious in World War II: the United States, the Soviet Union, Britain, France, and China (in 1971 the People's Republic of China replaced Nationalist China on the Security Council). In addition there are now ten rotating members—originally there were six.

It was deliberately set up so that the big powers could ignore any vote they didn't like. *Any one of the five permanent members of the Security Council can veto any enforcement action—even if the rest of the world is for it!* Since the Big Five have been behind most of the trouble in the world, it's like setting up the foxes to guard the chicken coop.

Because of the distrust and conflict between the Soviet Union and the United States (and because we usually vote to support our friends and they usually support their friends), deadlocks on all important issues involving war and peace have usually blocked effective action by the U.N. For example, the U.S. in 1990 vetoed a resolution for the U.N. to send a fact-finding mission to get information on the Jewish-Arab conflict in the occupied territories. An impartial understanding of what's happening is a needed first step in the peace process. This lack of respect for legal, peaceful conflict resolution has set a poor example for the other nations of the world.

Brian Urquhart, U.N. under secretary-general for special political affairs, lamented, "There are moments when I feel that only an invasion from outer space will reintroduce into the Security Council that unanimity and spirit which the founders of the Charter were talking about." Let us hope that the shock of Iraq's invasion of Kuwait and the threat to Saudi Arabia will begin to do it for us!

Thus we have a toddling Security Council that under the Charter is empowered to send armed forces anywhere on earth to stop war. And it is usually rendered impotent because of the Charter requirement for the unanimous vote of the permanent members

> *A Security Council that can be rendered impotent by the vote of one nation obviously cannot begin to guarantee security. A General Assembly that can pass resolutions with the votes of nations representing less than 10 percent of the world's population, and some 3 percent of the gross world product, will not have, and cannot get, the respect it must have if its decisions are to be taken seriously.*
>
> Dr. John Logue, Director
> Common Heritage Institute
> "A More Effective United Nations"
> *New Jersey Law Journal*
> December 26, 1985

of the Security Council to act in preserving peace. In 1945 we weren't quite ready yet to take the final step. Perhaps we're now waking up to the idiocy of living in an ungoverned world!

The General Assembly

In addition to the Security Council, the Charter of the United Nations set up the General Assembly. It has been called a "town meeting of the world" by former Secretary-General Trygve Lie. Each nation has one vote in the General Assembly, which has grown from the original 50 nations to 160 today. Thus small nations, *regardless of size*, have the same vote as large nations, *regardless of population*. For example, Grenada with about 90,000 people has an equal vote with the United States, which has 1/4 billion people.

Since the Security Council has all the power to act, the big powers gave the other nations of the world the power to talk! It's interesting to note that when a resolution passes the General Assembly, it goes to the Security Council *as a recommendation only*. The General Assembly has no Charter power to require any action to keep the peace—or to do anything but suggest!

Thus we are heading for the 21st Century with 160 "loose cannons" in the world. "But the hard fact remains," comments Richard Hudson in his newsletter *Global Report*, "that the decision-making system in the world body is too flawed to deal with the awesome gamut of our planet's problems in the coming decades. It is neither morally right or politically sensible to leave veto power in the Security Council in the hands of the five nuclear powers. It is plainly absurd to have decisions made on the basis of one nation, one vote in the General Assembly, thus giving countries with minute populations and minuscule contributions to the U.N. budget the same influence in decision-making as the bigger countries that have to pay the bills. Moreover, a central global decision-making body that can pass only non-binding recommendations is not what the world needs for the 21st century."

> *As Secretary General of this organization, with no allegiance except to the common interest, I feel the question may justifiably be put to the leading nuclear powers: By what right do they decide the fate of all humanity?... No one can expect to escape from the catastrophic consequences of a nuclear war on the fragile structure of our planet. The responsibility assumed by the Great Powers is now no longer to their populations alone; it is to every country and every people, to all of us.*
>
> Javier Pérez de Cuéllar,
> U.N. Secretary General
> December 1984

The Need for Reform

Patricia Mische, co-founder of Global Education Associates, tells a story that compares the United Nations to a dog that is expected to give protection from thieves and murderers. The dog is a good dog, but it has three problems. First, the masters muzzle the dog so the dog can bark but not bite, and thieves and murderers know this. Second, the masters don't feed the dog very well, so the dog is always hungry and anxious for itself, and lacks energy to do its job well. Third, the dog has 160 masters, and they often give conflicting directions and confuse the dog.

> The cause of the United Nations is inseparable from the cause of peace. But we will not have peace by afterthought. If the United Nations is to survive, those who represent it must bolster it, those who advocate it must submit to it, and those who believe in it must fight for it!
>
> Norman Cousins, President
> World Federalist Association
> Author, *Anatomy of an Illness*

Here is the prescription for rebuilding the UN: **Remove the muzzle, feed the dog, and reform the masters,** so they will not be confusing the dog.

Vernon Nash wrote in *The World Must Be Governed,* ". . . if Hamilton or any other founding father returned to the United States today and read a current article about the performance and prospects of the United Nations, he certainly would say to himself, 'This is where I came in.' . . . Then, as now, men kept trying to get order without law, to establish peace while retaining the right and power to go on doing as they pleased."

The United States, which was the principal mover in creating the World Court, gave the appearance of accepting compulsory jurisdiction over "any question of international law." But that was quite deceptive. By special reservations, the U.S. excluded certain types of disputes, which the U.S. could *by itself* decide it wanted solely within its own domestic jurisdiction.

A nation undermines the Court when it gives the appearance of accepting the Court and, at the same time, denies to the tribunal the normal powers of every judicial agency. *A nation that defies the jurisdiction of the Court when it becomes a defendant shows contempt for the Court.* A nation that ignores the Court when it doesn't like a judgment against it undercuts the process of law. When these things are done by the U.S., which helped establish the World Court, it diminishes respect for itself.

> *The United Nations is an extremely important and useful institution* provided *the peoples and governments of the world realize that it is merely a transitional system toward the final goal, which is the establishment of a supranational authority vested with sufficient legislative and executive powers to keep the peace.*
>
> Albert Einstein

Despite technical legal arguments that were raised to justify the U.S. position when Nicaragua in 1984 complained that we were mining its harbors and seeking to overthrow its government, the fact is that the U.S. refused to honor the Court or its judgments. This was seen throughout the world as a hypocritical manifestation of scorn for the tribunal—which the United States praised when decisions went in its favor. *Defiance of law is an invitation to disaster. What may have been tolerable in the prenuclear age is intolerable now.*

In a world of law and order, aggressor nations should clearly be identified as outlaws for rejecting the rule of law. This is not to suggest that justified grievances

94

should be ignored; sincere efforts must be made to find just solutions. *But a handful of states, or a small group of fanatics, should not be permitted to thwart humankind's progress toward a more lawful and peaceful world.*

Supporting the U.N.

In 1986 the U.S. Congress reduced its financial support of the United Nations by over half, largely because it did not like certain expenditures. Since the total U.N. budget is less than New York City's, any reduction of its annual $800 million income is crippling. In the past the Soviet Union has also failed to pay its U.N. dues for the same reason. In October 1987, Mikhail Gorbachev talked of invigorating the Security Council. To back up his words, the Soviet Union announced that it would pay all its overdue U.N. bills, which came to $197 million. And they've followed through on this promise.

> *World federalists are working for disarmament by seeking the ways to end all use of force in international relations. The only real alternative to war is an international legal system which provides common security for all states through the peaceful and just resolution of disputes according to law. This is vitally important in a world which has nuclear weapons. World federalists believe the test of sincerity of all who claim to want disarmament is their willingness to create and to be bound by a common world law and by agreed procedures for preventing aggression and solving conflicts peacefully.*
> **World Federalism**
> World Assoc. for World Federation

That left the United States in October 1987 the outstanding delinquent, who still owed over $414 million, including $61 million for peacekeeping forces that the U.S. opposed! As of December 1989, the U.S.

was behind $518 million—in violation of its treaty obligations. In his last budget request, President Reagan asked for full U.N. current funding and about a 10% payment on our past dues. Bush in his first budget made the same request. Our Congress was still unwilling to honor our obligations. The cost of only one Stealth bomber would cover our disgracefully broken contractual agreements with the U.N.—and with humanity's future.

The world spends only $800 MILLION a year on peace through the U.N., and about $1 TRILLION on national military budgets—**over a thousand times more!!!** Does it come as a surprise that we are today 1,000 times more effective at waging war than at waging peace?

> *We seek to strengthen the United Nations, to help solve its financial problems, to make it a more effective instrument for peace, to develop it into a genuine world security system . . . capable of resolving disputes on the basis of law, of insuring the security of the large and the small, and of creating conditions under which arms can finally be abolished . . . . This will require a new effort to achieve world law.*
>
> John F. Kennedy
> U.S. President

There are amazing parallels between our situation with the United Nations today and the dangerous situation in the United States two centuries ago. Tom Hudgens in his book *Let's Abolish War* points out that the Continental Congress under the Articles of Confederation:

1. Had no independent taxing powers.
2. Could not regulate interstate and foreign commerce.
3. Had no powers of direct enforcement of its laws.
4. Was ineffective in foreign affairs.

5. Had no chief executive.

6. Had no binding court of justice. . . .

"Do you realize," Hudgens asks, "that every one of these charges can be leveled at the United Nations today? We are living today under the Articles of Confederation except we call it the United Nations."

Instead of starting all over again, reforming the U.N. may be our best bet to rapidly ensure our ultimate human right. A redrafting of the Charter and its ratification by the nations of the world

> *The proposed system of comprehensive security will become operative to the extent that the United Nations, its Security Council and other international institutions and mechanisms function effectively. A decisive increase is required in the authority and role of the United Nations and the International Atomic Energy Agency.*
>
> Mikhail Gorbachev
> Soviet General Secretary
> Address to U.N., Sept. 1987

is needed. It won't be easy to persuade nations to mend their ways, but it can be done.

For years, the officials of the U.N. have known what needs to be done. They're powerless unless authorized by the nations of the world. They've been waiting for you to take the needed steps to alter the views of the entrenched diplomats, which would permit them to respond effectively to international lawlessness—and thus set the stage for a new era of prosperity and peace on earth.

Confederation vs. Federation

In order to take Step Five by working to make the U.N. more effective in the nuclear age, you must clearly understand the key differences between the U.N. today and the World Federation we need for tomorrow. Just as the terms "Confederation" and "Federation" were confusing to the 1787 delegates at Philadelphia, people usually don't understand their significance today. The World Federalist Association in its pamphlet *We the People* helps us clarify the crucial differences between a league or confederation, and a federation or union:

- In a league or confederation (like the U.N.), each state does as it pleases regardless of the consequences to the whole; in a *federation* or *union* (like the U.S.), each state accepts some restrictions for the security and well-being of the whole.

- In a league, the central body is merely a debating society without authority to control the harmful behavior of individuals; in a *federation*, the central body makes laws for the protection of the whole and prosecutes individuals who break them.

- In a league, any enforcement is attempted only against member states; in a *federation*, enforcement of laws is directed against *individual* lawbreakers.

- In a league, conflicts among members continue unabated, resulting in costly arms races and wars; in a *federation*, conflicts among states are worked out in a federal parliament and in federal courts.

- A league has no independent sources of revenue; a *federation* has its own supplemental sources of revenue.

- In a league, state loyalty overrides loyalty to the wider community; in a *federation*, loyalty to each state is balanced by loyalty to the wider community.

Finding the Best Way

Could you feel secure if a congress made up of people from all over the world enacted binding international laws? Would you be taken advantage of? Too heavily taxed? Your rights ignored? Could a dictator grab power? Can we set up a world legislature, court, and executive branch that will be more protective of the U.S. than the Pentagon? How can we actually increase our "defense" through a reformed U.N.? How do we reform the U.N. to avoid ecocide?*

As George Washington and Benjamin Franklin would testify, there is no one simple way to hammer out a new constitution. It takes an open-minded willingness to consider all points of

> *This planet is in bad political shape and is administered appallingly. An outer-space inspection team would undoubtedly give us an F (failure) or a triple D (dumb, deficient and dangerous) in planetary management. Our world is afflicted by a good dozen conflicts almost permanently. Its skies, lands and oceans are infested with atomic weapons which cost humanity 850 billion dollars a year, while so many poor people are still dying of hunger on this planet. And yet, I have seen the UN become universal and prevent many conflicts. I have seen the dangerous decolonization page turned quickly and with infinitely less bloodshed than in Europe and the Americas in preceding centuries. I have seen a flowering expansion of international cooperation in thirty-two UN specialized agencies and world programs.*
>
> Robert Muller
> Former U.N. Assistant Sec.-Gen.

view, to lay aside one's prejudices and psychological certainties, and to be patient enough to listen and search until effective answers are found and agreed upon. Just

---

* Ecocide is the deliberate destruction of the natural environment, as by pollutants.

as success in 1787 required that various states be satisfied, in like manner we must create a reformed U.N. that meets today's needs and interests of the nations of the world.

There have been many proposals to improve the United Nations and make it more effective as the keeper of the peace. One suggestion, known as the "Binding Triad," comes from Richard Hudson, founder of the Center for War/Peace Studies. It requires two basic modifications of the U.N. Charter:

> The voting system in the General Assembly would be changed. Important decisions would still be adopted with a single vote, *but with three simultaneous majorities within that vote.* Approval of a resolution would require that the majority vote include two-thirds of the members present and voting (as at present), nations representing two-thirds of the population of those present and voting, and nations representing two-thirds of the contributions to the regular U.N. budget of those present and voting. Thus, in order for a resolution to pass, it would have to be supported strongly by most of the countries of the world, most of the population of the world, and most of the political/economic/military strength of the world.
>
> The powers of the General Assembly would be increased under the Binding Triad so that in most cases its resolutions would be binding, not recommendations as at present. The new General Assembly, now a global legislature, will be able to use peacekeeping forces and/or economic sanctions to carry out its decisions. However, the Assembly would not be permitted "to intervene in matters which are essentially within the jurisdiction of any state." If the jurisdiction were in doubt, the issue would be referred to the World Court, and if the court ruled that the question was essentially domestic, the Assembly could not act.*

* For more information and a videotape on the Binding Triad, write the Center for War/Peace Studies, 218 E. 18th Street, New York, NY 10003. Phone: (212) 475-1077.

This is only one possibility for giving the General Assembly limited legislative powers. A World Constitution for the Federation of Earth has been drafted by the World Constitution and Parliament Association headed by Philip Isely of Lakewood, Colorado.* There are many ways to reform the U.N. to give the world binding international laws, a binding court of international justice, and an executive branch to enforce the law with effective economic sanctions and an international military force *that replaces national armies, navies, and air forces.*

A 14-point program is shown on the next page. Models of new international systems to create world order have been prepared by many scholars, among whom are Professor Richard Falk of Princeton University, Professor Saul Mendlovitz of Rutgers, and Professor Louis Sohn of Harvard University. With wise checks and balances, we can set up an overall system that will enable the world to work! Political leaders lack the political will to make the required changes in the U.N. It's time for the public to speak out.

> *There is enough bad in people to make world federal government necessary, and there is enough good in people to make it work.*
> Source Unknown

Once the world union is formed, do we want to permit an easy divorce if a nation wants to get out when it disagrees about something? The American Civil War in 1861–1865 settled whether states could leave the federal union if they disagreed with its policies. The victory by the Union clearly established that no state could secede from the federal government once it agreed to be a member.

* The address of the association is given in Appendix 1.

A 14-POINT PROGRAM
for Reforming
the United Nations

1. Improve the General Assembly decision-making process.

2. Modify the veto in the Security Council.

3. Create an International Disarmament Organization.

4. Improve the dispute settlement process.

5. Improve the U.N.'s peacekeeping capability.

6. Provide for adequate and stable U.N. revenues.

7. Increase the use of the International Court of Justice.

8. Create an International Criminal Court to try hijackers and terrorists.

9. Improve the U.N.'s human rights machinery.

10. Create stronger U.N. environmental and conservation programs.

11. Provide international authorities for areas not under national control.

12. Provide for more effective world trade and monetary systems.

13. Establish a consolidated U.N. development program.

14. Achieve administrative reform of the U.N. system.

For more information, write to Campaign for U.N. Reform, 418 Seventh Street, S.E., Washington, DC 20003. Phone: (202) 546-3956.

If politicians in a nation become angry and could whip up the people to get out, it would signal the end of the world system. Once a nation agrees to the reformed U.N., it must be permanent. "By resigning from the organization," Cord Meyer warns, "a nation could free itself from international supervision, forcing a renewal of the arma-

> *Many of these proposals may appear unpatriotic or even treasonous to those who identify patriotism with the worship of American military power. . . . If patriotism is an active concern for the freedom, welfare and survival of one's people, there is no patriotic duty more immediate than the abolition of war as a national right and institution.*
>
> Cord Meyer
> Peace or Anarchy

ment race and certain war. In view of the nature of the new weapons, secession would be synonymous with aggression."*

As we've pointed out, *there is no one way* to transform the United Nations into an effective world government. It is important that you give thought to this vital matter and arrive at your own conclusions on how to do it. Then discuss them with your friends and neighbors, who will no doubt develop their own ideas. It is only from the clash of opinions that a living truth will emerge that will point to an effective way to complete the governmental structure of the world.

The Challenge of Our Age

We are at a crucial point in history. We are on the threshold of great progress. We have reached the stage

---

* After World War II, the Soviet Union took over Lithuania by military conquest—not the free vote of the people. You will recall that the Philadelphia Constitutional Convention in 1787 clearly specified that the vote of the *people*—not the politicians—was required to join the United States of America. Lithuania's desire today for independence is not considered aggression.

where large-scale wars are no longer compatible with the future of the human race. We have gone beyond the point where such military power is protective. Instead it threatens to kill us all. We are gradually fouling our environment so that it cannot support human life. And we now know that we must have global institutions to solve our global problems.*

"Environmental knowledge and concerns," according to Pamela Leonard, "have risen at an increasingly rapid rate in recent years, and many nations have enacted laws and set up agencies to deal with them. Yet little has been done to create laws or institutions on an international scale, despite the fact that the impacts of air and water pollutants travel as easily across national boundaries as across municipal boundaries."**

> *Let us also think about establishing an emergency environmental aid centre within the U.N. Its function would be to promptly dispatch international groups of experts to areas that have experienced a sharp deterioration in the environmental situation.*
>
> Mikhail Gorbachev
> Soviet General Secretary
> Address to the U.N., New York
> December 7, 1988

Increasing Abundance

Even if we were not threatened by nuclear war or environmental ruin, we would benefit enormously by a reformed U.N. Through a world republic, our children will have greater prosperity, more personal opportunities for a good life, better maintenance of our

* Pace Law School in White Plains, New York has a Center for Environmental Legal Studies headed by Professor Nicholas A. Robinson. He teaches lawyers about environmental problems now facing our nation and the world.
** From *Effective Global Environmental Protection* by Pamela Leonard. Published by World Federalist Association, May 1990.

precious planet, and better protection of their human rights and freedoms.

Imagine what a difference this would make in your life and that of your loved ones. The heavy taxes that spill your "economic blood" year by year would no longer be used to feed a greedy war machine. Your children could then feel confident that they would have a future. Business could be liberated from the import and export fences that limit opportunities. We could effectively begin to improve the quality of the air we breathe and the water we drink. Education, medical care, and quality of life would vastly improve when the world no longer spent $1.5 million each minute on increasing its killing capacity. *A small international peacekeeping force of several hundred thousand well-trained and equipped people could replace the millions of soldiers now under arms who constantly disrupt the peace of the planet.*

> *It is dangerous, in the most literal sense of the word, when streams of poison flow into the rivers, when toxic rains fall on the earth from the sky, when towns and entire regions are suffocating in an atmosphere saturated with the fumes put out by industry and by vehicles, when the development of nuclear power is accompanied by unacceptable risks.*
> Mikhail Gorbachev
> Soviet General Secretary
> Address to U.N., Sept. 1987

Over the past several centuries there has been a gradual awakening to the importance of international law that can override the military passions of the 160 separate nations around the globe. We have tried world courts and have found that they work if we want them to. We have set up international organizations such as the League of Nations and the United Nations. Each has been a step forward.

PRESERVING
THE GLOBAL ENVIRONMENT

Prepared by the World Resources Institute, Washington, DC, and the American Assembly, affiliated with Columbia University, founded by Dwight D. Eisenhower in 1950.

Three indivisibly linked global environmental trends together constitute an increasingly grave challenge to the habitability of the earth. They are human population growth; tropical deforestation and the rapid loss of biological diversity; and global atmospheric change, including stratospheric ozone loss and greenhouse warming. These trends threaten nations' economic potential, therefore their internal political security, their citizens' health (because of increased ultraviolet radiation), and, in the case of global warming, possibly their very existence. No more basic threat to national security exists. Thus, together with economic interdependence, global environmental threats are shifting traditional national security concerns to a focus on collective global security.

The degradation of the global environment is integrally linked to human population growth. More than 90 million people are added each year—more than ever before. On its present trajectory, the world's population could nearly triple its current size, reaching 14 billion before stabilizing. With an heroic effort, it could level off at around 9 billion. However, today's unmet need for family planning is huge: only 30 percent of reproductive age people in the developing world outside of China currently have access to contraception. Women's full and equal participation in society at all levels must be rapidly addressed.

Tropical deforestation and the loss of a diverse set of species rob the earth of its biological richness, which undermines long-range ecological security and global economic potential. Nearly 20 million hectares of tropical forests are lost every year. Conservative estimates put the extinction rate at one hundred species per day: a rate unmatched since the disappearance of the dinosaurs. Escalating human populations, deforestation, disruptions of watersheds, soil loss, and land degradation are all linked in a vicious cycle that perpetuates and deepens poverty, and often creates ecological refugees.

The depletion of the ozone layer by chlorofluorocarbons (CFCs) allows increased ultraviolet B radiation from the sun to enter the earth's atmosphere, threatening human health and the productivity of the biosphere.

There is a scientific consensus that rising concentrations of greenhouse gases will cause global climatic change. Atmospheric levels of carbon dioxide have increased 25 percent since the beginning of the industrial era.

Therefore, the earth is set to experience substantial climate change of unknown scale and rapidity. The consequences are likely to include sea level rise, greater frequency of extreme weather events, disruption of ecosystems, and potentially vast impacts on the global economy. The processes of climate change are irreversible and major additional releases could be triggered from the biosphere by global warming in an uncontrollable self-reinforcing process (e.g. methane release from unfrozen Arctic tundra).

We call attention to the need for immediate international action to reverse trends that threaten the integrity of the global environment. These trends endanger all nations and require collective action and cooperation among all nations in the common interest. Our message is one of urgency. Accountable and courageous leadership in all sectors will be needed to mobilize the necessary effort. If the world community fails to act forcefully in the current decade, the earth's ability to sustain life is at risk.

Excerpt from *Preserving the Global Environment: A Challenge of Shared Leadership*. New York: W.W. Norton & Company, 1990.

All this experimenting, testing, trying, and hoping *have been important steps up the ladder of international growth* toward the completion of the governance of our world. We now have the glorious challenge of creating lasting peace and prosperity by reforming the United Nations into a world republic.

Approaching Planethood

Many nations today, and eventually all nations, will be willing to cooperate in a reformed United Nations. They will respond to the insistence of their people that we do not let our planet be ruined or blown apart through war. These nations will want to benefit from the much safer and far less costly protection of their national rights and freedoms that *only a world government can offer them.*

> *A federation of all humanity, together with a sufficient means of social justice to ensure health, education, and a rough equality of opportunity, would mean such a release and increase of human energy as to open a new phase in human history.*
>
> H.G. Wells
> Noted Historian

At long last, the people of this world can get out of the arms race and enjoy a much higher standard of living, environmental protection, education, culture, medical care, etc. We need a world governance that, unlike the present Security Council, cannot be vetoed by one of the five victorious nations of World War II. It will be able to effectively respond to environmental problems that threaten the security of everyone everywhere.

It is now time for the people to insist on reforming the U.N. Charter. They will become a powerful force when they *unite and act together.* Sooner or later, those who resist at first will join in—

just as holdout states discovered *they could not afford to pass up the many benefits* of becoming a part of the United States two centuries ago.

The draft of the U.N. Charter was discussed at Dumbarton Oaks, a private estate in Washington, DC. On a tablet in the garden was inscribed a prophetic motto: "As ye sow, so shall ye reap." When the final instrument was accepted by 50 nations on June 26, 1945, everyone knew that it was less than perfect. The Secretary of State reported to President Truman: "What has resulted is a human document with human imperfections but with human hopes and human victory as well."

We need a new "Dumbarton Oaks" to draft the changes required by the 21st Century. On December 23, 1987, our Congress passed a law calling for the appointment by our President of a bipartisan U.S. Commission to Improve the Effectiveness of the United Nations. Commissioners should have been appointed by June 1, 1989. By August 1990 there was still no indication that our President would comply with this law of Congress. Let the voice of the people be heard!

> *With all the positive news that's coming from Eastern Europe and the U.S. government about significant nuclear arsenal reductions (as much as 50%), it's easy to get lulled into complacency about the nuclear arms race. But consider this: the U.S. is still building and testing nuclear weapons and their delivery systems. We are still building the ultimate doomsday device known as Star Wars. Even with these reductions in our arsenals, the U.S. and Soviets will still have enough firepower to blow the world up 5,000 times, not to mention the French, Israeli or Chinese stockpiles (as well as the rest of the world). And what about all the toxic wastes? Where will the madness end?*
>
> Richard Gold
> Eugene PeaceWorks
> Eugene, Oregon

109

Send a copy of *PlanetHood* to the President and to your congressional leaders. Tell them you're tired of delay and indecision. If they get flooded with reminders from the voters, they'll soon take notice. It is time to act NOW so that the dreams of the U.N. founders may finally become a reality.

We can no longer pretend that we don't know what needs to be done. How long will it be until a president, prime minister, or general secretary calls for a Conference to Reform the United Nations or an International Constitutional Convention—and invites all nations to send delegates? Here is an opportunity for statesmanship and fame of the highest order. Let us seize this history-making opportunity and accept the challenge to create a more peaceful world.

Like Paul Revere, let's awaken our neighbors. Let's give ourselves effective international law, world courts, and enforcement in a safe system of checks and balances. Let's work continuously to bring about the day when our front lines of defense consist of brigades of international attorneys practicing before a binding world court. Then we'll have finally secured our ultimate human right to live in dignity in a healthy environment free from the threat of war.

> *The founding of the United Nations embodies our deepest hopes for a peaceful world. And during the past year, we've come closer than ever before to realizing those hopes. We've seen a century sundered by barbed threats and barbed wire, give way to a new era of peace and competition and freedom.*
>
> *This is a new and different world. Not since 1945 have we seen the real possibility of using the United Nations as it was designed, as a center for international collective security.*
>
> George Bush
> U.S. President, October 1, 1990
> Address to the United Nations

We need a reliable cop on the international corner. Will you help our ungoverned world to create a world system that can work?

You'll be taking the Fifth Step toward planethood when you play your part in making the U.N. effective for the 21st Century. As a Planethood Patriot, you'll know that you are

> *Environmentalists and politicians can argue the costs and benefits of international action on global warming from now until doomsday, and they probably will. But nothing will get done without an institutional mechanism to develop, institute and enforce regulations across national boundaries.*
>
> Elliot Richardson
> Head of the U.S. Delegation
> Law of the Sea Conference

doing what you can to make your life count. You will have saved yourself, your family, and all of the men, women, and children throughout our beautiful planet— now and for generations to come.

IT DEPENDS ON YOU!

6th Step

Tell Your Friends and Neighbors

To rescue yourself and your family, it is important that you tell the great news to your friends and neighbors: *a safe way has been found to get rid of mass killing machines and protect the environment.* By reforming the United Nations with improved international law, courts, and enforcement, we can give all people on Planet Earth *a level of military and environmental security that we lack today.*

You can help people understand that all of us are citizens of the world— as well as citizens of our own city, state, and nation. Perhaps they already realize that today's fifty thousand nuclear devices do not give us security—instead, they are the greatest danger humanity has ever known. It's good news that an improved world system *will make it safe* to eliminate the arms race, which costs about $1.5 million per minute worldwide. We should all make sure that our tax dollars are used for the benefit—and not for the death—of society.

> *It is strange: one could not envisage for a moment a household, a city, a school, a firm, a factory, a farm, an institution, a religion, or a nation without a head, a principal, a manager, an administrator, or a government. But we accept readily that the world can be left without one! We should not be surprised, therefore, that there are so many wars, acts of violence, and global crises on this planet.*
>
> Robert Muller
> Former U.N. Assist. Sec.-Gen.

For every billion dollars spent on death devices, we create about 28,000 jobs. That same amount of money could create 71,000 jobs if spent for education, and 57,000 jobs if used to buy goods and services. Economist Robert W. Reuschlein tells us, " . . . each one percent of GNP (gross national product) spent on the military reduces manufacturing productivity by one percent." He continues,

> . . . great nations decline when they arrogantly overmilitarize trying to maintain control of the world with force. Large standing armies eat into economic growth reminding us of complaints about King George's army "eating out our sustenance" as references in our Declaration of Independence indicate. These declining powers cling to their military burdens even when they are economically drowning in them. Power tends to corrupt; absolute power corrupts absolutely. Pride, especially national pride, comes before a fall. The sword cuts many ways, especially economically, in the saying "live by the sword and die by the sword." This is not altogether new, except that the causal agent has been plainly located thanks to modern economic information and data collection.*

Surely, it is in everyone's interest to spend money for living rather than dying. Few people understand the great abundance we can create when we get rid of our dependence on costly killing machines. There is incredible

> There is deception and mismanagement at the highest levels in the Department of Defense.
> Senator Lowell Weicker, Jr.
> Ranking Republican
> Senate Appropriations Com., 1987

waste (as well as corruption) in the production of redundant military systems for overlapping military services.

According to Rear Admiral Gene R. LaRocque, U.S. Navy (Ret.), "Weapons are often purchased primarily for the benefit of major military contractors, not for the

---

* From *Peace Economics: Newest Scientific Proof That Military Spending Causes Decline* by Robert W. Reuschlein.

114

WHY IS AMERICA DECLINING?

Now that we know military spending causes the decline and fall of nations, what are some of the typical symptoms in this rise and fall scenario? When the economy was abundant and the society was growing, it needed everybody and every idea possible to meet all the new challenges economically. Workers are respected then and school kids study harder. There is less escapism, because reality is so much more stimulating, less crime because job opportunities are everywhere.

When the society stops growing as it once did, the formerly expanding economic pie begins to tighten. Declining nations syndrome sets in with rising unemployment, inflation, and crime. The mentality of the whole society starts changing as quick fixes, cheating, and elbowing others aside become the ways to get more out of the shrinking pie. Politics and power plays become the ways to get ahead in the stagnant economy. . . . Drugs and alcoholism are on the rise as we look to escapism. We look more to celebrities for escape and for some hope in a hopeless situation and are apathetic in our politics, as we feel less powerful and less in control of our lives. We cling to the past and our former glories as the system becomes more rigid and entrenched in its ways.

Health care expenditures tend to be less in the world's more militarized societies and prison rates are the highest in the world in Russia, America, and South Africa, the two armed camps and an internally militarized society. Crime went up after the Vietnamese war ended as . . . battle-scarred and scorned veterans returned home to joblessness, suicide, and depression. Studies have shown how this has led to increased crime, along with the baby boom reaching the prime crime years of 18 to 30 years old.

Taken from *Peace Economics: Newest Scientific Proof That Military Spending Causes Decline*, Robert W. Reuschlein, P.O. Box 10083, Eugene, OR 97440.

defense of the United States. In the absence of effective competition in the military industry, the profit motive gives companies the incentive to sell as many weapons at as high a price as possible." Furthermore, much of the world's scientific brain power is being squandered on weapons of mass destruction, instead of being used for vital human betterment.

In 1988, *The Strategic Cooperation Initiative,* written by Air Force Major General Jack Kidd (Ret.), denounced the folly of Star Wars. General Kidd tells us, "Ending the arms race, eliminating nuclear weapons, reducing other armaments, and reversing the degradation of world environment are imperative actions which must be accomplished for our physical, economic and mental well-being and, indeed, our very survival. The great question before our nation is whether we have the foresight and fortitude to intelligently manage our way out of problems which we, ourselves, have created."*

> *Teach your children what we have taught our children, that the Earth is our mother. Whatever befalls the Earth, befalls the children of the Earth. This we know. The Earth does not belong to us; we belong to the Earth.*
>
> Chief Seattle

Both Dr. Helen Caldicott and President Dwight Eisenhower put the blame for our nuclear madness on what political scientists call the Iron Triangle—the military, the politicians, and the industrialists who profit in the millions or billions. The responsibility should *also rest with each of us who neglects to do what we can to correct the situation.*

*The Strategic Cooperation Initiative by Jack Kidd, Major General, U.S. Air Force (Ret.). Charlottesville: Three Presidents Publishing Company, 1988.

The military is only doing what it's trained to do. Commanders must assume that "the enemy" intends to attack. Naturally, they want more and better weapons all the time. A good way to get more is to publicly underestimate their own strength while exaggerating that of their adversary.

Human beings forget to be human. It is up to YOU to make it clear to people around you that war is not a glorious game and a "casualty" is not merely a statistic. It is YOUR son, YOUR daughter, YOUR husband, YOUR wife, YOUR friend, and YOU! When the military asks for billions of dollars of your money for a weapon of mass destruction, demand to know how many *people* it will kill and *who* those people are likely to be, and *why* they deserve such a fate. Insist upon an answer. If you don't care enough to act, you must share the blame.

The U.S. military purse is controlled by the Congress, and Congress is controlled by the people.

> *World government is not an "ultimate goal" but an immediate necessity. In fact, it has been overdue since 1914. The convulsions of the past decades are the clear symptoms of a dead and decaying political system.*
> Emery Reves
> *The Anatomy of Peace*

It is up to *you*, the informed voters, *to stop robbing the hungry and the poor to feed an insatiable war machine.* Between 1960 and 1980, worldwide military expenditures nearly doubled. The expenditure curve for arms is ever upward. World military budgets now exceed TWO BILLION DOLLARS EACH DAY! What is so ironic and tragic is that these enormous military expenditures do not enhance national security—they undermine it. There can be no winner of a nuclear war; everybody loses and loses everything.

117

The Strength of a Nation

The strength of a nation does not depend solely upon its capacity to destroy other nations and kill their citizens. True national security is dependent upon the spirit of its people, their respect for the integrity of their leaders, and their confidence in the justness of their government. When people are lied to or taken advantage of, the government will lack their respect and lose power—despite the vastness of its military arsenal. As long as significant portions of the population feel that they are mere pawns in a dangerous costly game of the politicians, the military, and the industrialists, the vital stamina, unity, and determination of the nation will be destroyed.

Imagine what would happen if the world were blessed with leaders who were determined and able to implement the declared goal of complete disarmament under effective international controls. *Imagine the savings being used to retrain displaced workers, stimulate new industries, protect the environment, get rid of national debt and deficits, lower taxes, control the drug trade, and improve housing, education, and medical care—and to help raise the standard of living in underdeveloped countries.*

> *Don't trust government statements. They fit the facts to fit the policy.*
> William J. Fulbright
> Former Chairman, U.S. Senate
> Foreign Relations Committee
> On his 80th birthday

The great reduction of military expenses (made possible by a reformed U.N. capable of maintaining peace in the world) could quickly wipe out the U.S. budget deficit. We could then begin to pay off our enormous national debt. And it could enable us to gradually reverse our big trade deficit by producing better civilian products instead of better ways to kill off humanity. It would enable the Soviets to produce more consumer goods and thereby serve their own people better. As we've mentioned, Japan, *whose Constitution prohibits massive armaments*, has risen from the ashes of defeat in World War II to demonstrate that today economic power is more important than military power.

> *The exercise by some nation-states of their as-yet-unlimited right to lie, assassinate, terrorize and wage war, and to justify these actions in the name of "national security," causes many to despair for the future of our planet. But there is a solution to this problem of international anarchy: A common security system for all nations under enforceable world law.*
>
> Myron W. Kronisch
> Campaign for U.N. Reform

Since the consequences of disarmament are so obviously desirable from every point of view, it is an insult to human intelligence to believe that such reasonable goals are unattainable. If we are to dwell together in peace on this interdependent planet, traditional perceptions of self-interest based on military power must be relegated to a bygone age. *All humankind must be brought under the protective shield of an enlightened planethood.*

Solving International Problems

It is important that your friends and neighbors understand that the preservation of our planet for human habitation requires that we add a final layer of international government to get rid of the international anarchy we have today. *International problems must have international solutions.*

119

Here is a partial list of the challenges we face that can be solved **only** by international laws, courts, and enforcement:

- Millions killed by ongoing wars.
- Intolerable military budgets that impoverish the citizens of the world.
- International terrorism.
- Acid rain from one country that destroys forests in neighboring nations.
- Nuclear pollution of the air. (It is known today that everyone on earth now has tiny amounts of radioactive nuclear particles in his or her body from the debris of bomb tests, the escape of radioactive materials into the air, etc.)
- The destruction of the oceans and marine life.
- Contagious and infectious diseases that spread across national borders—such as AIDS.
- Ravaging the planet's minerals, oil supply, and other natural resources.
- Tariffs and regulations that impede the flow of goods and services internationally.
- The greenhouse effect and the depletion of the ozone layer, which sustains life on earth.
- The destruction of the rain forests that produce oxygen for us to breathe and are a biological gold mine.
- Overpopulation that strangles the earth.

This interdependent world cannot function effectively without international cooperation and a willingness to give and take. A world republic can increase educational, cultural, and business opportunities for people throughout the globe. It can sponsor the cooperative exploration of the frontiers of space. *It can enable our human dreams to come true.*

A New Era of Human Happiness

Robert D. McFadden, writing in the *New York Times* on April 23, 1990, described a new kind of war. "Millions Join Battle for a Beloved Planet," said the front-page headline. The *Times* reporter described how "millions of people around the nation and the world

> We are facing problems that transcend nations. When we talk about the greenhouse effect, we are talking about something that affects not just the United States or Brazil but the entire planet.
> Isaac Asimov
> Author of 400 books

renewed the call to arms for an endangered planet yesterday with an exuberant and bittersweet celebration of Earth Day 1990."

An estimated 200 million people from 140 nations have taken part in the largest grassroots demonstration in history. Ordinary people turned away from the fearful memories of cold war confrontation to join in vast throngs to deliver a peaceful message to their political leaders. In Kiev, a young survivor of the Soviet nuclear accident at Chernobyl carried a sign saying "Down with Radiation!" 5,000 people in Italy lay down on the roadway to protest car fumes. A 500-mile long human chain stretched across France. "It's really necessary to start saving the earth," said Kathy Bernstein, 60, at a festival in Chicago. "I'm here because an individual can make a difference," said Leslea Meyerhoff, 22, at a rally in Los Angeles. In Washington, 125,000 people crowded the Capitol Mall while a throng of 750,000 jammed New York's Central Park. In London, Andrew Lees declared: "It will give the clear message to politicians that millions of people are aware of the problems facing the earth and what needs to be done about it."

We can help our friends understand that planethood *for the first time* will enable all people to enjoy the abundance that modern technology can provide—instead of the curse of modern war that threatens to kill us. It can open up a new era in the unfolding of the

121

creative, artistic, and spiritual potentials that lie within all of us. It can enormously increase our level of happiness and well-being upon this earth. And planethood can help us save the biosphere from destruction.

It is important for all of us to realize that the true patriots of today must look at the world with an international breadth of mind. The "life, liberty, and pursuit of happiness" set forth in the Declaration of Independence in 1776 can only be attained in the 21st Century through the completion of a new world structure. These "inalienable rights" do not belong only to Americans. *They belong to everyone on this planet.*

> *The popes of the nuclear age, from Pius XII through John Paul II, have affirmed pursuit of international order as the way to banish the scourge of war from human affairs.*
> Pastoral Letter
> U.S. Catholic Bishops, 1983

The patriots of the 21st Century will be those who realize that human survival is a race between planethood and military and/or environmental catastrophe. Since you now possess this knowledge and understanding, it is your responsibility to pass on a new global view of humankind. This is our Sixth Step toward planethood. You can begin today to tell your friends and neighbors of the enormous benefits of planethood. We must help those whose thoughts are still stuck in the "Wild West" ruts of settling problems by mass killing.

International anarchy, NO.
Law and order, YES!

7th Step

Do Your Daily Deed for Planethood

We have seen that after the horrors of each world war, nations recognized—at least for a brief time—that change was necessary to create a peaceful world order. World War I produced the Covenant of the League of Nations; World War II gave us the U.N. Charter. Both contained high ideals and the implied promise that war would be outlawed. Those in authority knew what was required; it had been carefully set forth for years by competent, dedicated political experts. *The truth is that our political leaders simply did not dare enough—or care enough. We, the public, did not do enough. We all let each other down.*

> We need first and foremost a world democracy, a government of this planet for the people and by the people. But the problem is so colossal and unprecedented that few political thinkers even dare to consider it. They feel more at ease discussing the number and strength of missiles needed to protect specific national corrals. Since government and institutions are so slow and reluctant to do it, we must build the world community through individual commitment and action.
>
> **Robert Muller**
> **Former U.N. Assistant Sec.-Gen.**

In today's fast-moving world, important decision makers have little time to think. Since government leaders are thus far unable to meet the challenge of creating a peaceful world, it is up to you and other people of vision to take action to achieve the necessary reforms. *Remember, if the people lead, the leaders will follow.*

125

Amazing Progress

After more than forty years of antagonism, the United States and the Soviet Union are finally beginning to overcome their fears and prejudices. The Russians have recognized that their planned economy cannot satisfy the needs of their citizens; they now eagerly seek cooperation with the previously reviled capitalists. McDonald's sells hamburgers in Moscow! No longer does our President call the Soviet Union an "evil empire." At the U.N., on September 25, 1989, President Bush referred to "a new attitude that prevails between the United States and the U.S.S.R." He has repeatedly declared that he wished success to Soviet leader Gorbachev.

> The idea of a comprehensive system of security is the first plan for a possible new organization of life in our common planetary home. In other words, it is a pass into our future where security of all is a token of the security for everyone. We hope the current session of the United Nations General Assembly will jointly develop and concretise this idea.
>
> Mikhail Gorbachev
> Soviet General Secretary
> *Pravda*, September 17, 1987

The Soviet Union has called for a new comprehensive system of international peace and security. On September 17, 1987 Gorbachev in *Pravda* acknowledged that our diverse world is interlinked and interdependent. He called for international cooperation in all fields: military, political, economic, ecological, and humanitarian. He stated that disarmament is a desired goal, including the elimination of all foreign bases and the recall of Soviet troops from Afghanistan. He advocated respect for the U.N. Charter and stronger monitoring to avert wars. He called for international verification of arms limitation treaties (as the U.S. has demanded). He reaffirmed the right to live in dignity and the importance of international law and order. He even referred to giving binding jurisdiction to the International Court of Justice (usually called the World Court).

This plan was presented to the United Nations. Said Mr. Gorbachev, "The imperatives of the moment call on us to raise many of the principles of everyday common sense to the level of policy." Finding the world threatened with destruction, the Soviet leader put his finger on the main point: "Nothing will change unless we start to act."

The United Nations was thrilled to hear Gorbachev proclaim on December 7, 1988 that the Soviets would, unilaterally, start massive reductions of their military forces. Mass emigration of dissidents and freedom of expression has become a reality in the Soviet Union. For the first

> *It is difficult to think of anything that would put the United States in a stronger world position than for it to become the champion of a program to rebuild the United Nations into a true world order.*
> Norman Cousins, President
> World Federalist Association
> Author, *Anatomy of an Illness*

time in its history, it accepted the compulsory jurisdiction of the International Court of Justice for six human rights conventions. Deputy Foreign Minister Petrovsky declared on October 6, 1989, "Only legal order and self-restraint through international law can ensure a positive evolution of the world. . . . No alternative exists to an organization of relations among states based on law."

These changes have made *peaceful coexistence*— and indeed peaceful *cooperation*—possible. WE CAN BE FRIENDS. On November 3, 1989 U.S. Assistant Secretary of State John Bolton referred to a "new spirit of constructive cooperation" as the U.S. and the Soviet Union introduced a joint resolution adopted by the U.N.

for "enhancing international peace, security, and international cooperation in all its aspects."

Instead of sending Russian tanks to suppress people seeking freedom from communism as had been the practice in the past, Gorbachev declared on December 11, 1989 that East European countries are entitled to "sovereignty, noninterference and freedom of choice." Without the use of massive arms, these nations are moving toward democracy.

> If people get hungry enough, they'll reach for almost anything. Of the 120 wars fought in the past 40 years, over a hundred were fought in Third World countries— by people who could no longer feed their families. Some were forced off their land by resettlement programs. Some were driven into urban slums when they couldn't make money on their crops. Others simply could not afford to buy food when prices tripled overnight.
>
> Interfaith Hunger Appeal

We are recognizing that the *strength of a nation* cannot rest only on its military might. We are moving toward a rational approach to solving international problems by building *a new era of human well-being.* It's as though the world's leaders had read and were beginning to understand the ideas of *PlanetHood!*

The goals advocated by the Soviet leader in his new policy of openness are goals that the United States has always cherished. If the U.S. is to remain a world leader, it must not hesitate to lead. If the leaders won't lead, let the people lead—and the "leaders" will have to follow. It's up to us!

Your Daily Deed

Since we don't know how much time we have before today's unstable environmental and military situation explodes on us, we must move rapidly. More and more nations are building nuclear missiles and making poison gas. Our lives are at risk—a computer may give a false alarm, or a political or military fanatic may trigger a chain of events that cripples humanity. Let us resolve to create a chain of events that can save humanity.

To be a part of a chain of events to give yourself the benefits of planethood, we suggest that you pledge to yourself and the world to do a daily deed: a daily action that will bring world governance a tiny step closer. You'll be a planethood patriot helping to replace the *law of force* with the *force of law.*

Such a Planethood Patriot pledge need not be burdensome. Depending upon your time and money available, you can live out your pledge *with integrity each day* on either a maximum or a minimum basis— or something in between. For example, as a daily deed you could write a letter to a friend about U.N. reform. Or you could phone a friend and discuss what you can do to help bring about U.N. reform and other needed changes.

> *If we fail to seize the moment, history will never forgive us—if there is a history.*
> Thomas A. Watson, 1987
> Former U.S. Ambassador
> to Moscow

changes. You might donate $1.00 or more to one of the organizations working for U.N. reform listed in Appendix 1 or to any other organization working for planethood.

Remember the amount is not as important as *doing something every day.* You might choose to give this book to at least one person per day. With your neighbors you could divide a shipment of 1,000 books in the mass market size, which can be purchased for the nonprofit price of only 50¢ each postpaid. (See Page 191.) Then all you'd have to do is hand out one *PlanetHood* each day or leave one in a public place such as a doctor's office, an airport lounge, or someone's doorstep. You could offer this book to a passerby on the street, mail it to a friend or relative, or send a copy to influential people in the news (libraries can furnish you with addresses from reference books).

You may choose to photocopy the Proclamation Form provided in Appendix 4. Then for your daily deed for peace, you could gather signatures from people who wish to assert their Ultimate Human Right. Then mail them to the U.N. and your chosen politicians. If done day by day, this could have a great synergistic impact! John Holden of Washington, DC, got over 2,000 people from 90 countries to sign the *PlanetHood* Proclamation, "My Ultimate Human Right." (See Appendix 4.)

> So there's an understandable tendency to think that the problem of nuclear war has been solved, or at least is being solved—that we can now ignore it and turn our attention to the formidable array of other pressing problems. This opinion is surprisingly widespread. It is, we believe, a dangerous illusion.
>
> Carl Sagan and Richard Turco
> *Too Many Weapons in the World*

Your daily contribution can be done in a way that gives you a satisfying feeling that your energy is really helping to give humanity a future. If your funds are minimal at this time, *each day* you can put at least one cent into a box labeled "Planethood." If this is all you could contribute daily, over a period of a year it would total $3.65. Even this amount would help a group to promote a world system of governance. If you are fortunate enough to have more money and view this donation as *an investment in your future,* you might donate a percentage of your income to helping the cause of permanent peace, plenty, and preserving the planet. After all, of what use is your money if the world goes down the drain in the next few years?

For each tax-deductible donation of $3, a copy of the pocketbook edition of *PlanetHood* will be mailed anywhere in the U.S. and the world using carefully selected mailing lists, or we'll use any mailing list you send us. (See page 191.) You may wish to organize fund-raising activities to get donations for this important activity. To be tax deductible, checks should be made out to The Vision Foundation (Planethood Program), 700 Commercial Avenue, Coos Bay, OR 97420.

The important thing is to resolve to do your daily deed for planethood. And since the need is urgent, we suggest that your commitment to yourself and the world be for seven days a week—52 weeks in the year until world governance is achieved. Your helping the world has great consequences, and you can do it as an enjoyable project that deeply builds your self-esteem and feeling of patriotism.

You can avoid treating those who disagree with you as an enemy. You can learn to increasingly keep your

> "Tell me the weight of a snowflake," a robin asked a wild dove.
>
> "Nothing more than nothing," was the answer.
>
> "In that case I must tell you a marvelous story," the robin said. "I sat on the branch of a fir, close to its trunk, when it began to snow—not heavily, not in a raging blizzard, no, just like in a dream, without any violence. Since I didn't have anything better to do, I counted the snowflakes settling on the twigs and needles of my branch. Their number was exactly 3,741,952. When the next snowflake dropped onto the branch—nothing more than nothing, as you say—the branch broke off." Having said that, the robin flew away.
>
> The dove, since Noah's time an authority on the matter, thought about the story for a while and finally said to herself: "Perhaps there is only one person's voice lacking for peace to come about in the world."

heart and mind open. You can disagree without being disagreeable—and at the same time do what you know is necessary to save humanity. You can rearrange the priorities in your life so that you are a real power for rescuing humanity.

As modern Planethood Patriots, we can pick the activities for which we have the most energy. And although dedicated, we can maintain a reasonable balance so that we do not neglect our jobs or families in ways that undermine the wholeness of our lives. If all of us follow through on the commitment of one deed for planethood each day, the job will get done. As Aesop's fable showed, the race was not won by the rabbit who traveled in great spurts; it was won by the tortoise who kept going and going and going. . . .

> *Blessed are the peacemakers: for they shall be called the children of God.*
>
> Christ
> Sermon on the Mount

Wage Peace—Not War

Planethood means learning to think in terms of a new world system of governance rather than "defense" or military systems. We must all strive to create a community consciousness on the global level. We must take care of our planetary home. It's the only one we have. Perhaps you will want to organize a local U.N. reform group or join an existing organization. You could contact one of the organizations listed in Appendix 1 and find out how you can support its activities.*

You could play a part in helping the people of this earth become acquainted with each other. Traveling

* There are many excellent books. You could start with *50 Simple Things You Can Do to Save the Earth* by the EarthWorks Group. Berkeley: Earthworks Press, 1989.

in foreign lands as a planethood ambassador for friendship and community can be an interesting way to follow through on your daily commitment. Cultural and educational exchanges, and sharing scientific, business, and vocational skills can help correct false images that may have been created by their politicians or ours in the past.

Whenever you notice folks from another country visiting your city, you might ask if they're aware of the work now being done to support a new approach to solving the world's problems. Almost everyone appreciates friendly, caring energy when they are in a foreign land. They might also furnish you with names of people in their nation you can write to as your daily deed for planethood.

> A change in public opinion is always the first condition for a change in institutions. Our tragedy is that the power of the press, radio and television is used exclusively to propagate disarmament, alliances, deterrents, containments, nonaggression pacts and other treaty arrangements which, in our time and age, are thoroughly irrelevant and outdated. There can be no doubt that, if it were possible to clarify the fundamental principles of peace through the mass media, to discuss its meaning and how to obtain it, an overwhelming majority of mankind would enthusiastically endorse policies and measures integrating the sovereign nation-states into a higher legal order.
>
> Emery Reves
> *The Anatomy of Peace*

Many exchanges are taking place. For example, there are regular private meetings in Moscow between American and Soviet lawyers. In June 1990, the Pace Peace Center started a dialogue between U.S. and Soviet international lawyers to build the new legal structures for a peaceful planetary world order.

American and Soviet doctors researching the medical problems of nuclear fallout have shared a Nobel

Prize. Soviet and American astronauts have in the past gone into space together. Private American citizens have joined Soviet scientists to set up seismic tests to measure nuclear blasts. Americans are now cruising down the Volga River, while Russians are boating down the Mississippi. There is a "Kids-to-Kids" exchange. The Association for Humanistic Psychology organized a people-to-people exchange of letters and snapshots with folks in the Soviet Union. Such friendly and constructive contacts can lead to improved human-to-human feelings and understanding.

Educate for Peace

As part of your daily deed for planethood, you might check on what your local elementary schools, high schools, and colleges are doing to create a global vision. Literature classes can read about war and peace; philosophy classes can examine

> To reach peace, teach peace.
> Pope John Paul II

the ethics of nuclear deterrence; and psychology, economics, and social science classes can examine the human and social costs of warfare. History classes can study what has and hasn't worked in the past to keep peace among nations. Music classes can learn to sing anthems not only for nations, but for all humankind. The problems of war and peace and global community touch every field of study. The senior author has established an interdisciplinary Peace Center at Pace University Law School, where he teaches the International Law of Peace.

"A total of 235 U.S. institutions of higher learning," according to the World Policy Institute, "were offering majors, minors or concentrations in peace studies during the 1986–87 academic year; and 46 percent of all U.S.

colleges and universities taught at least one course in the field, up from 14.6 percent in 1979. Professors Betty G. Lall and Lyn Fine of New York University published a reference guide in 1988, listing over 500 graduate courses in peace taught at 19 schools in the New York Metropolitan area alone.*

Students on all levels must be helped to develop factual, informed, and ethical perceptions regarding international problems. They must understand the responsibilities of being citizens in a world experiencing massive technological, economic, and political transitions. *They must learn that there are life-expanding alternatives to the present system of armed violence and environmental apathy.* Our young people are the seeds, the promises that can grow into the world community leaders of tomorrow.

Make It Happen

The moral and ethical teachings of religious groups of all faiths must become a part of our reeducational process for planethood. ("Thou shalt not kill." "Love one another.") Our personal ideas of serving Jesus, God, or Allah must not mislead us into blowing up the planet and killing everyone. Instead, in the name of that which is holy to each of us, let's open our hearts and create peace on earth with goodwill toward all.

* Many excellent learning and teaching tools have been published by Professors Burns II. Weston at the University of Iowa; Richard A. Falk and Johan Galtung of Princeton University; Saul Mendlovitz of Rutgers University; Kenneth and Elise Boulding of the University of Colorado; Anthony A. D'Amato of Northwestern University; Dietrich Fischer of Princeton and Pace Universities; Carolyn Stephenson of University of Hawaii at Manoa, Honolulu; Betty Reardon, Teachers College, Columbia University; John Whitely of the University of California at Irvine, California; and the World Policy Institute, 777 U.N. Plaza, New York. All these scholars are teaching the advantages of an alternative security system based on ridding ourselves of world anarchy and settling disputes without killing people.

135

A 1983 pastoral letter of U.S. Catholic Bishops, and a similar letter issued by Methodist Bishops in 1986, called for a reformed international structure to meet the needs of the nuclear age. The popes of the nuclear age, from Pius XII through John Paul II, have affirmed the pursuit of international order as the way to banish the devastation of war.

> *Resolve that to insure world peace and disarmament among nations, we United Methodists of the Rocky Mountain Conference urge the President and the Congress of the United States, in concert with all other willing nations, to call a World Constitutional Convention to reform the United Nations into a federal, representative world government* . . . .
> United Methodist Church, 1983
> Rocky Mountain Conference

There must be an end to the glorification of killing and violence. The young should not be taught to kill for old slogans. ("My country right or wrong, but right or wrong, my country.") Children must learn that it is far nobler to live for humankind than to die for the glory of a particular ruler, nation, or sect. Visiting heads of state could be greeted not by the traditional twenty-one gun military salute, but by songs and flowers.

All the modern means of molding public opinion—the schools, religious institutions, TV, radio, newspapers, and magazines—as well as private organizations and individuals—must get on the new bandwagon to accelerate our world along the path of planethood. We can have great influence when we are carried forward by a determination to create a peaceful, healthy planet for our children.

The creative minds of people everywhere can rapidly begin to develop a passion for planethood. Within less than a year we can create a grassroots groundswell to reorganize our international relations so that we may all live in peace and dignity. The genius of the human intellect and the caring in our hearts will find the most suitable solutions. Through your pledge to yourself that you'll not go to sleep any night until you have completed your daily deed for planethood, you can help it all happen in time.

Trade and Aid

No nation wishes to antagonize or go to war with an important trading partner on whom its own welfare depends. Japan and the Federal Republic of Germany were enemies of the United States not too long ago. Today we are all customers of each others' goods, and the ties of friendship and alliance are strong.

Howard Brembeck (Founder and Director of Chore Time-Brock, Inc., a farm equipment manufacturer in Milford, Indiana) is deeply concerned by the danger to humanity. In his book, *The Civilized Defense Plan,* he shows how international trade can be used to deter and stop aggression. He suggests that all law-abiding nations simply refuse to trade with law-breaking nations.

Thus trade can be used as a weapon for peace. He spells out

> *I like to believe that people in the long run are going to do more to promote peace than are governments. Indeed, I think that people want peace so much that one of these days governments had better get out of their way and let them have it.*
> Dwight D. Eisenhower, 1959
> U.S. President

step by step how this can be accomplished globally to create a peaceful and prosperous planet. When Iraq invaded Kuwait on August 1, 1990, President Bush instantly cut off all trade with Iraq in response to the mandate of the Security Council of the U.N. This was a small step in the direction advocated in Brembeck's plan.

Aid to countries in need can add to international goodwill. Whether it be disaster relief or financial aid to developing countries, *both the recipient and the donor can acquire a sense of kinship* in the knowledge that they are participating in the enhancement of human community, caring, and dignity. Let's stop using aid primarily for increasing killing power and creating military alliances. Let the human heart be our guide.

Speak and Act for Planethood

Never underestimate the power of the determined individual! The inspiring example of Mahatma Gandhi's courageous and successful stand against the British empire is well-known. Civil rights and women's rights have been achieved because people had the courage to speak out. Young people in the United States proved that they could change the course of a war by peaceful protests against the inhumanity of the Vietnam war. "Hell, No! We Won't Go!" became a rallying cry that helped end a war.

> *These weapons of mass destruction can, at the press of a button, erase people of a whole nation or a whole continent, in just a matter of minutes.... With these weapons available to any dictatorial government headed by a Hitler, a Stalin, a Tojo, a Franco, a Salazar, a Khomeini, Castro, Noriega, Hussein or Qaddafi, where is the hope for freedom from fear for people of the world? The reality is we are still slaves to an outdated concept of world power.*
> Howard S. Brembeck, Author
> The Civilized Defense Plan
> President, Fourth Freedom Forum

Each concerned citizen has a role to play. What that role may be will depend upon individual interests and skills. Some may only be able to express an opinion in private. Others may write a letter, sign a petition, or write a book. You may choose to lead or join a march, make a speech, or teach a class. You may wish to join one of the organizations listed in Appendix 1.

A noted California attorney, the late Frank Stark, and Carlyn, his dedicated wife, toured America in a van while speaking on U.N. reform along the way. Captain Tom Hudgens flies across the country distributing his exciting book, *Let's Abolish War: We Need L.A.W.* It passionately pleads for world government. Pediatrician Dr. Alfred W. Bauer of Kirkland, Washington asks each of his patients to read *PlanetHood* because "the health of your children depends on it."

Annie Marquier-Dumont has produced a beautiful French edition of *PlanetHood*. It is titled *PlanetHood ou les Citoyens du Monde* and is available from Les Éditions Universelles du Verseau, C.P. 1074, Knowlton, Quebec, Canada J0E 1V0.

Many celebrities campaign for peace. Famous pediatrician and octogenarian, the late Dr. Benjamin Spock, was arrested for peace when he climbed over fences of missile sites, which he felt threatened genocide; Barbra Streisand sings for peace; actor Paul Newman speaks for peace; Yehudi Menuhin plays his violin for peace. Gregory Peck starred in a movie about peace called *Amazing Grace and Chuck*. Daniel Ellsberg, former Pentagon official, today works for peace. Garry Davis, son of a famous bandleader, earned worldwide notoriety when he declared himself a "world citizen" and issued thousands of "World

> *Our goals are those of the U.N.'s founders, who sought to replace a world at war with one where the rule of law would prevail, where human rights were honored, where development would blossom, where conflict would give way to freedom from violence.*
>
> **U.S. President Ronald Reagan**
> Address to the U.N.
> September 26, 1983

Government" passports. However, when planethood arrives, world citizen passports will not be needed— unless you travel to the Moon or Mars!

Some run for peace; some march for peace. Mayor Larry Agran of Irvine, California heads a coalition of a thousand local officials organized to demand that funds be allocated to cities rather than wasted on armaments. He and Michael Shuman head the Center for Innovative Diplomacy, 17931 Sky Park Circle, Irvine, CA 92714. They publish the *Bulletin of Municipal Foreign Policy,* which notes the impact of foreign policy decisions on local communities.

> *The United Nations will have to be reformed or it will collapse into total irrelevance and nuclear war will follow.*
> Carlos P. Romulo, 1984
> Phillippine Statesman

In September 1989, Dick Trostler, inspired by *PlanetHood,* published a booklet, *World Peace Now,* which can be ordered from him at 976 W. Foothill Blvd., Suite 426, Claremont, CA 91711. It's an easily understandable booklet explaining planethood and can be read in less than an hour.

Network for Peace

Throughout the world, thousands of organizations, institutions, and private groups of various sizes and strengths are dealing with problems of peace and planethood. *They are springing up like antibodies created by nature to cure a sick organism. They need all the help they can get if the patient is to survive.*

The Consortium on Peace Research, Education and Development (COPRED), George Mason University, Fairfax, VA 22030, provides linkage and information to hundreds of members throughout America. Global Education Associates, 475 Riverside Drive, New York,

NY 10115, led by Patricia and Gerald Mische, authors of the inspiring book *Toward a Human World Order,* contribute hope and information in a broad area. Many women's and church groups actively pursue goals of planethood and peace.

A growing number of institutions in Europe, India, and Asia are dedicated to helping humanity create a better future. Foundations and individuals support the evolution of our world community. The United Nations University began operating in Tokyo in 1975. The University for Peace was established in Costa

> *Recent history suggests that military powers—regardless of ideology—will take constructive steps toward global security only if an energetic public, in many parts of the world, insists that together we subordinate the pursuit of national power and wealth to the call for human survival and dignity.*
>
> Robert C. Johansen, 1984
> World Policy Institute

Rica in 1983. Its unpaid Chancellor is our friend Robert Muller, who wrote our Foreword. The Peace Institute in honor of President Harry Truman operates at the Hebrew University in Jerusalem.

In 1985, the U.S. Congress established the United States Institute of Peace, which has been providing grants from public funds for research on peace and conflict resolution. The Canadian government now sponsors the very promising Institute for Peace and Security. Computer technology is just beginning to pull the peace net together.

In February 1989, there was an unprecedented convocation in Washington, DC. Some 1,400 persons from over 100 cosponsoring organizations met to hear over 80 prominent speakers address the issues of global security in the 1990s. Sarah Harder, president of the American Association of University Women, and the

Rev. William Sloane Coffin, president of SANE/FREEZE, co-sponsored the impressive event. The participants each received a free copy of *PlanetHood*. One of the principal organizers and fund-raisers was Stanley Platt, a retired businessman in Minneapolis. A follow-up conference in November 1989 formed the Alliance for Our Common Future, to work for "a just world community, healthy global environment and effective structures for peace." Membership is open to all. Simply write care of National Peace Institute Foundation, 110 Maryland Ave., N.E., Washington, DC 20002.

> *All truth passes through three stages.*
> *First, it is ridiculed.*
> *Second, it is violently opposed.*
> *Third, it is accepted as being self-evident.*
> Arthur Schopenhauer

These loose strands now floating on a vast sea must be strengthened, drawn together, and woven into more effective networks if we are to catch the prize of planethood.

Your personal commitment to a daily deed for planethood can make the difference between our planet's surviving or not surviving. How you think about our world community and your own daily deeds will be noticed—and will inspire other people. Just as hate is transmitted from person to person like a virus, feelings of planethood with understanding, heart-to-heart cooperation, and caring are also very contagious. From your life activities, your energy can inspire others and thereby multiply a thousandfold as you fulfill your daily commitment to yourself and to the world.

Think globally—act locally. It's up to you! You can empower yourself to play your part in saving the world!

8th Step

*Give Yourself
a Planethood
Prize*

The eight steps we've formulated to avoid the destruction of our species will take time and patience. But do we have any other way? As each of us realizes that our energy and personal power are essential to creating planethood through world law, we can feel that our lives are beginning to count in the most threatening crisis that has ever faced humankind. We're beginning to understand:

If it is to be, it's up to me!

It is within your power to save the world for yourself, your family, your friends, and all the people yet to live. You'll deserve a Planethood Prize if you help to replace our perilous international anarchy with a limited system of international governance with checks and balances.

Goals of Government

We have seen that humankind is not simply moving in a vicious tailspin; instead it is on *an upward climb* toward completing the governmental structure of the world. We are inspired by our great progress toward planethood.

What do we want from our governments—whether city, county, state, national, or international? *We want them to shield us from harm, protect our rights and freedoms, and make it possible to live in a degree of health, comfort, and dignity.*

A government must be neither too weak nor too strong. It must be designed to be fair and impartial so that both minorities and majorities realize that they are better off to rely on laws and courts than to use violence—even though they don't always get what they want when they want it.

> I believe the best approach to ending the arms race is to educate the public about the pocketbook issues talked about in this work. If they know that unprecedented prosperity exceeding even that of the sixties has been foregone in order to impose military might on the Third World, and that we are endangering our standing among the nations, I don't think they will stand for it anymore.
>
> Robert W. Reuschlein
> Author, *Peace Economics: Newest Scientific Proof That Military Spending Causes Decline*

The Founding Fathers of the United States in 1787 invented a new form of federal government that *combines* existing state governments with an overall federal governing power. *Since the U.S. federal government can enforce its laws by direct action against individual citizens, it does not have to depend on the states or declare war on a state in order to enforce a policy for the common benefit of all.* It can simply punish individual wrong-doers that have violated a federal law. We now use this ingenious political structure that has worked for two hundred years to govern as many as fifty states from Florida to Alaska to Hawaii.

The U.S. federal government in coordination with city, county, and state governments all supplement each other to protect our rights as citizens to enjoy the highest level of freedom consistent with the freedom of others. We can similarly design our international government so that it is equally protective of our freedom *as individuals and as nations.*

A world court can settle disputes between nation-states and also guarantee that each nation will retain the right to decide matters that affect its own people within its own borders. Through planethood, each of the 160 nations on earth can enjoy the safety of being a member of a larger international community with laws, courts, and enforcement *that can give them more security than they now have*—and much more prosperity and other good things in life.

We are smart enough to create an

> *Our current generation is committing Treason against future generations by destroying our global Environment . . .*
> Norman Cousins, President
> World Federalist Association
> Author, *Anatomy of an Illness*

improved international system with checks and balances and a division of power that can make us safe from a dictator's getting control. For 200 years, the U.S. has proved that a properly drawn constitution can do this. We can build our future by learning from the mistakes and successes of the past. As day follows night, we have the power to move from the present darkness into the sunlight.

Toward a Governed World

The world is changing because the present system doesn't work. Unbridled sovereignty is being gradually restricted by the need for coping with common problems on a global basis. We're becoming aware of the sacred whole of our wonderful world. (See "Interdependence of World Problems" on the next page.)

Binding rules are already governing some of the environment and outer space. New international tribunals are settling a host of problems by lawful means. The processes of mediation and conciliation are being improved. Both inside and outside the United Nations, the need for U.N. reform has been recognized and is being slowly implemented. It is up to you to increase the grassroots people-to-people support of U.N. reform

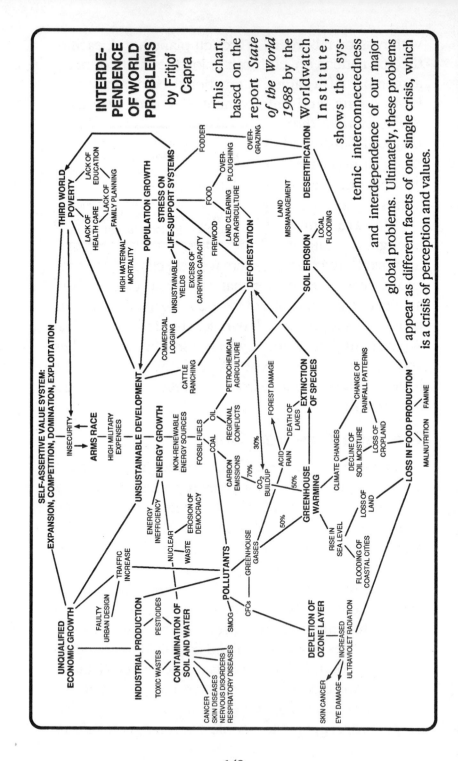

INTERDEPENDENCE OF WORLD PROBLEMS
by Fritjof Capra

This chart, based on the report *State of the World 1988* by the Worldwatch Institute, shows the systemic interconnectedness and interdependence of our major global problems. Ultimately, these problems appear as different facets of one single crisis, which is a crisis of perception and values.

SELF-ASSERTIVE VALUE SYSTEM:
EXPANSION, COMPETITION, DOMINATION, EXPLOITATION

THIRD WORLD POVERTY

LACK OF EDUCATION
LACK OF FAMILY PLANNING
LACK OF HEALTH CARE
HIGH MATERNAL MORTALITY

POPULATION GROWTH

STRESS ON LIFE-SUPPORT SYSTEMS

FODDER
OVER-GRAZING
OVER-PLOUGHING
FOOD
DESERTIFICATION
LAND CLEARING FOR AGRICULTURE
FIREWOOD
LAND MISMANAGEMENT
EXCESS OF CARRYING CAPACITY
UNSUSTAINABLE YIELDS
SOIL EROSION
LOCAL FLOODING

INSECURITY

ARMS RACE
HIGH MILITARY EXPENSES

UNSUSTAINABLE DEVELOPMENT

ENERGY GROWTH

NON-RENEWABLE ENERGY SOURCES
FOSSIL FUELS

COMMERCIAL LOGGING
CATTLE RANCHING
PETROCHEMICAL AGRICULTURE

DEFORESTATION

FOREST DAMAGE
DEATH OF LAKES
EXTINCTION OF SPECIES

CHANGE OF RAINFALL PATTERNS
LOSS OF CROPLAND
CLIMATE CHANGES
DECLINE OF SOIL MOISTURE

LOSS IN FOOD PRODUCTION
MALNUTRITION   FAMINE

ENERGY INEFFICIENCY
EROSION OF DEMOCRACY
NUCLEAR
WASTE

OIL
COAL
REGIONAL CONFLICTS
30%
70%
CO2 BUILDUP
ACID RAIN
50%

CARBON EMISSIONS

GREENHOUSE WARMING

RISE IN SEA LEVEL
LOSS OF LAND

50%
GREENHOUSE GASES

UNQUALIFIED ECONOMIC GROWTH

FAULTY URBAN DESIGN
TRAFFIC INCREASE

INDUSTRIAL PRODUCTION
PESTICIDES
CONTAMINATION OF SOIL AND WATER

POLLUTANTS

SMOG
CFCs

DEPLETION OF OZONE LAYER

FLOODING OF COASTAL CITIES

TOXIC WASTES
CANCER
SKIN DISEASES
NERVOUS DISORDERS
RESPIRATORY DISEASES

SKIN CANCER
EYE DAMAGE
INCREASED ULTRAVIOLET RADIATION

148

so that it may remove the "need" for the wasteful "defense" expenditures that are costing the people of this world a million and a half dollars per minute. *Unless we destroy all weapons of mass destruction, the weapons will destroy us all.*

In "Reality and Guarantees for a Secure World" published in *Pravda* on September 17, 1987, Mikhail Gorbachev wrote:

> I do not venture to foretell how the system of all embracing security would appear in its final form. It is only clear that it could become a reality only if all means of mass annihilation were destroyed. We propose that all this be pondered by an independent commission of experts and specialists, which would submit its conclusions to the United Nations Organization. . . .

We stand on the brink of great new solutions. The Soviet Union, the United States, and other countries are beginning to realize that something must be done—urgently and quickly. We must replace fear with action that builds confidence. As former U.S. President Franklin D. Roosevelt said in another context, "We have nothing to fear but fear itself."

> *World Government is not only possible, it is inevitable; and when it comes, it will appeal to patriotism in its truest, in its only sense, the patriotism of men who love their national heritages so deeply that they wish to preserve them in safety for the common good.*
>
> Peter Ustinov
> Renowned Actor

Although the lights of progress may sometimes flicker, the trend toward an integrated, coordinated, and more humane world is clearly discernible to the penetrating eye. Noting the unprecedented strides toward world law made during this century, we should recall that *each one was a step taken for the first time since humans began to walk the face of the earth.*

Exaggerated emphasis on the frailties of the present U.N. encourages unjustified cynicism and skepticism. It erodes the public confidence needed to stimulate the improvements that are required. We must take heart from our accomplishments—and never lose faith because of temporary defeats. There is much to be done. *Complacency and leaving the job to others can snatch defeat from victory.*

Winding Down the Arms Race

We cannot stop an arms race without halting the production of arms. Since our supply of killing machines can already destroy more people than the number of human beings available to be killed, it makes no sense to continue to expand the superfluous destructive capacity. The history of the world shows that when politicians and the military spend large amounts on armaments, their minds will somehow sooner or later find an excuse to use the killing machines for "defense." We must go beyond the ancient theory that the only way to achieve peace is to hold a big gun to someone's head!

> *There is no salvation for civilization, or even the human race, other than the creation of a world government.*
> Albert Einstein

If nuclear weapons are not usable because they will destroy all civilization, it is fair to ask: "Of what use are such unusable weapons?" The theory of deterrence is based on the logic that if nations remain vulnerable, they are safe because neither side can afford to attack first—mutual assured destruction. But countless wars show how the military becomes overconfident.

Our security cannot be allowed to depend upon a war system that is suicidal. Those who support the argument that armaments are essential for deterrence often cite the Latin maxim: "If you want peace, prepare for war." But ancient Rome did not anticipate the nuclear age and environmental destruction. History shows that those who prepared for war usually got what they prepared for.

IF YOU WANT PEACE, PREPARE FOR PEACE!

Exercise Your Political Muscle

Most important: Use your political power! What every person in a democratic society can and must do is: VOTE, VOTE, VOTE! This great privilege of democracy is too often left unused. Persistent expressions of concern, wrath, or anguish from voters carry enormous weight in the halls of Congress. You may wish to nominate and elect candidates on the basis of their policies for planethood. Ideologues of narrow vision who believe a better world can be built by the arrogant brandishing of military might should be voted out of office. Young people who today may not be motivated to vote must learn that they can make a difference, and that there is a future for them.

> *We live on a planet that is terminally ill . . . . The United States has lost its direction and its soul. Use your democracy to save your world.*
>
> Helen Caldicott, M.D., 1986
> Former President, Physicians for Social Responsibility

Many political leaders believe that refusal to make concessions is evidence of strong character, which will endear them to their constituents and coerce their opponents. They mistake stubbornness for strength and fail to perceive the needs of the 21st Century. They mislead rather than lead the people they hope to protect. If those in high office are unwilling or unable to demonstrate the flexibility required to protect the future of humankind, every peaceful effort should be made to replace them.

> *Details are not crucial; the important point is to find a plan for peace that would be both effective and generally acceptable. If a sufficient effort is made, the effective wisdom of mankind can find the right combination.*
> Dr. Louis Sohn, 1982, Coauthor
> *World Peace Through World Law*

Many organizations keep track of the voting records of all members of Congress. Their reports will show which members are voting for billions of taxpayers' dollars for increased killing capacity instead of measures that support planethood objectives. As informed citizens, we must oppose everyone who slows down our progress toward a genuine world community. Every action that moves humankind toward the desired goal must be supported and encouraged. No political leader can ignore the sustained cry of the people.

Forward to Planethood

A handful of politicians, military leaders, and industrialists with narrow vision cannot be allowed to determine the fate of humankind. The earth may have begun with a big bang, but no one vested a few mortals with the right to decide that it should end the same way.

All the essential ingredients for a peaceful world are interrelated and linked. Progress in attaining one component stimulates acceptance of other components. Similarly, failure to advance in one area impedes progress elsewhere. Like the fingers of the hand, all the parts must move together in a firm and coordinated way.

No private citizen would surrender weapons if there were an armed and belligerent neighbor in an area where laws, courts, and police were nonexistent. So too, no nation can be expected to destroy all its military might as long as there are no other means for maintaining security, freedom, justice, and peace. If we wish to

> **PLANETHOOD PLEDGE OF ALLEGIANCE**
>
> *I pledge allegiance to the Earth, and to the planet for which it stands; one world, under law, indivisible, with liberty and justice for all.*
>
> Martin Hayes

stop the stockpiling of nuclear death, we must establish a world system where international law, courts, and enforcement are a reality.

Let's use whatever influence we have, and whatever strength we can muster, to make sure that current international problems are dealt with in ways that support the ultimate goal of planethood through world law. By doing our deeds for planethood, we can put the necessary parts in place so that the house of peace and planetary preservation will rest on a firmer foundation than it does today.

When he addressed the United Nations in 1984, President Reagan said:

> For the sake of a peaceful world, a world where human dignity and freedom is respected and enshrined, let us approach each other with tenfold trust and thousandfold affection. A new future awaits us. The time is here, the moment is now.

On April 10, 1987, Mikhail Gorbachev publicly accepted the idea of nuclear disarmament "under strict control" and verification. He called for a new social revolution by "the development of all forms of representative and direct democracy. . . ." His book *Perestroika: New Thinking for Our Country*

153

and the World (Harper and Row, 1987) concluded:

> We want people of every country to enjoy prosperity, welfare and happiness. The road to this lies through proceeding to a nuclear-free non-violent world. We have embarked on this road, and call on other countries and nations to follow suit.

President Bush, addressing the Congress on January 31, 1990, referred to "the Revolution of '89" and "changes so striking that it marks the beginning of a new era in the world's affairs."

"Our aim," Bush said, "[must be] to take the lead in forging peace and freedom's best hope, a great and growing commonwealth of free nations."

Today you have the greatest opportunity you will ever have to make your life deeply count to save yourself, your family, and the human species. It is an opportunity to stand tall with the good feeling that you are engaged in the *noblest purpose* that has ever motivated any human being in the history of the world. You can rededicate your life to the ideals of planethood: a global commonwealth that gives us freedom from war and a bountiful planetary home.

> *Let us resolve to bring our heroic energy together to build a new world that integrates the wisdom of the heart with the wisdom of the mind.*
>
> Ken and Penny Keyes
> *Gathering Power
> Through Insight and Love*

Never have you been challenged so profoundly. Never have you been given such a great opportunity to use all that is noble and good within you. Never have the stakes been so high in the game of life. Never have your efforts been more needed than at the present moment in world history. Never has the world been so dependent upon you.

Power lies with YOU. *We mean you.* After all the promises that have been made to you, all the beautiful words said by politicians, all the declarations that have been universally accepted, and with all the great promise of the 21st Century, it is time for you to assert your ultimate human right to live with dignity in a healthy environment free from the threat of war.

Planethood Is on the March

A new sense of world community is bursting on the international scene. Spurred by instant global communications, human beings everywhere are asserting—and attaining—their right to determine their own destiny in peace and dignity. The inability of the communist system to satisfy the economic and political needs of people under its control has led to its relatively nonviolent overthrow in Poland, Hungary, Czechoslovakia, Rumania, Bulgaria, Yugoslavia, and East Germany. The new revolution was fired by Soviet recognition that economic restructuring and "openness" were necessary for survival. Today, the communist world reaches out to the capitalist world for peaceful cooperation.

> *For I dipt into the future,*
> *   far as human eye could see,*
> *Saw the Vision of the world,*
> *   and all the wonder that would be; . . .*
> *Till the war-drum throbb'd no longer,*
> *   and the battle-flags were furl'd*
> *In the Parliament of man,*
> *   the Federation of the world.*
> Alfred, Lord Tennyson
> "Locksley Hall," 1842

Many wars have been brought to a halt, such as in Afghanistan and Nicaragua. In other areas, efforts have been intensified to curtail hostilities. Significant progress is being made. Some token nuclear weapons are being destroyed and the need to reduce arms is generally recognized. The injustice of apartheid in South Africa is being overcome. The United Nations is being strengthened, and there is a new opportunity for collective security to function as envisaged by the Charter. Perhaps Iraq's invasion of Kuwait will make us realize the stupidity of continuing the present world anarchy.

> *We are convinced that the comprehensive system of security is at the same time a system for a universal legal order which will ensure the primacy of international law in politics.*
>
> Mikhail Gorbachev
> Soviet General Secretary
> U.N. Address, September 1987

Disrespect for international law (while claiming noble goals) threatens us all. There are some who still equate military power with greatness and increased security. They fail to recognize that in the nuclear age military might *diminishes* security.

NO NATION CAN BE SECURE UNTIL ALL NATIONS ARE SECURE. The capacity to kill great masses of people cannot resolve problems. It can only intensify the human needs that still plague this planet.

Among the main enemies the world still faces today are fear, the continuing cost of armaments, lawlessness, poverty, racial and religious bigotry, hunger, homelessness, drug abuse, terrorism, AIDS, inadequate medical care, environmental pollution, inability to dispose of hazardous waste, illiteracy, population growth, foreign debt burdens, and disrespect for fundamental human rights. These common burdens cannot be overcome by more killing power. They can only be resolved by cooperative management on a planetary scale.

Let us therefore join together with renewed inspiration drawn from the enormous strides being made today—and the confidence that we can build a better tomorrow for everyone.

Let your planethood voice be heard—loud and clear throughout the world! You will become a Planethood Patriot bringing in a new era of world harmony. Through your dedication to this noble cause, you can award yourself a personal planethood prize for having done your best for your human family.

> *Recognition of the inherent dignity and of the equal and inalienable rights of all members of the human family is the foundation of freedom, justice and peace in the world.*
> Universal Declaration of Human Rights

Then we can all enjoy the greatest prize:

Peace on Earth!
Goodwill toward all!

EIGHT STEPS TO
PLANETHOOD

1. Insist on Your Ultimate Human Right
2. Understand What Needs to Be Done
3. Become a Planethood Patriot
4. Recognize Our Great Progress
5. Help Reform the U.N. for the Planethood Age
6. Tell Your Friends and Neighbors
7. Do Your Daily Deed for Planethood
8. Give Yourself a Planethood Prize!

Begin Today!

Appendix 1
Expanding Your Personal Power

To rescue yourself and all of humanity, it is important that you know what you are talking about. Simply being for peace and the environment and against war and ruin is not enough. To add to your life insurance for the 21st Century, you may wish to invest in the books below—and then absorb them as though your life depended on it—for it really does. You can also expand your personal power by writing for the literature of the organizations listed in this appendix.

To Increase Your Understanding

Your local library offers many resources on the transition from anarchy to law, courts, and enforcement. Here are some books that can give you a lot of information quite rapidly:

The Great Rehearsal: The Story of Making and Ratifying the Constitution of the United States by Carl Van Doren. New York: Viking Penguin, Inc., 1987. $6.95 in the paperback Penguin edition. This enjoyable book tunes you into the political wisdom, the attitudes of compromise, and the craftsmanship with which the founding fathers of the United States put the U.S. Constitution together. It gives you a front-row preview of what you need to do to support reforming the Charter of the United Nations. That's why it's called *The Great Rehearsal.*

World Federalist Bicentennial Reader compiled by Barbara M. Walker. Washington, DC: World Federalist Association, 1987. $5.00. This is a gold mine for deepening your understanding of the ingredients that go into building a successful constitution. It may be ordered directly from the World Federalist Association, 418 Seventh Street, S.E., Washington, DC 20003.

Beyond the Bomb by Mark Sommer. A perceptive guide to alternative strategies for peace; available in paperback from Talman Co., 150 Fifth Ave., NY 10011.

Winning Peace: Strategies and Ethics for a Nuclear Free World by Dietrich Fischer, Wilhelm Nolte, and Jan Oberg. Philadelphia: Taylor and Francis, 1989. Paperback.

One World: The Approach to Permanent Peace on Earth and The General Happiness of Mankind by John Kiang, a Chinese scholar's encyclopedic study of human evolution toward global peace. 1984. One World Publishing Company, P.O.B. 423, Notre Dame, IN 46556.

For Advanced Study

Here's a list of books by Benjamin B. Ferencz that spell out in detail the things we must do to establish a new international system to ensure world peace:

Defining International Aggression—The Search for World Peace: A Documentary History and Analysis by Benjamin B. Ferencz. 2 volumes. New York: Oceana Publications, Inc., 1975.

An International Criminal Court—A Step Toward World Peace: A Documentary History and Analysis by Benjamin B. Ferencz. 2 volumes. New York: Oceana Publications, Inc., 1980.

Enforcing International Law—A Way to World Peace: A Documentary History and Analysis by Benjamin B. Ferencz. 2 volumes. New York: Oceana Publications, Inc., 1983.

A Common Sense Guide to World Peace by Benjamin B. Ferencz. New York: Oceana Publications,

1985. $15 hardcover, $5 paperback. This book with fewer than 100 pages is in three parts: what *has* been done; what *should* be done; what *can* be done. It is packed with information.

Networking With Organizations

As a modern Planethood Patriot you may also wish to become a member of one or all of the following organizations, which are devoted to the cause of replacing the law of force with the force of law. They don't require it, but we suggest that you send them $2 to help cover postage and printing costs of the information they will send you. Both volunteer helpers and monetary contributions are urgently needed to do their noble work in time to save humanity:

WORLD FEDERALIST
ASSOCIATION
418 Seventh Street, S.E.
Washington, DC 20003
Phone: (202) 546-3950
1-800-HATE WAR

CAMPAIGN FOR U.N.
REFORM
418 Seventh Street, S.E.
Washington, DC 20003
Phone: (202) 546-3956

CENTER FOR
WAR/PEACE STUDIES
218 East 18th Street
New York, NY 10003
Phone: (212) 475-1077

CONSORTIUM ON PEACE
RESEARCH, EDUCATION,
AND DEVELOPMENT
(COPRED)
George Mason University
4400 University Drive
Fairfax, VA 22030
Phone: (703) 323-2806

WORLD ASSOCIATION
FOR WORLD FEDERATION
Leliegracht 21, 1016 GR
Amsterdam, The Netherlands
Phone: (020) 227502
or
United Nations Office
777 United Nations Plaza
New York, NY 10017
Phone: (212) 599-1320

WORLD CITIZENS
ASSEMBLY
2820 Van Ness Avenue
San Francisco, CA 94109
Phone: (415) 474-9773

20/20 VISION
69 So. Pleasant St., #203
Amherst, MA 01002
Phone: 1-800-347-2767

PARLIAMENTARIANS
GLOBAL ACTION
211 East 43rd Street, Suite 1604
New York, NY 10017
Phone: (212) 687-7755

GLOBAL EDUCATION
ASSOCIATES
475 Riverside Drive
New York, NY 10115
Phone: (212) 870-3290

UNITED NATIONS
ASSOCIATION—U.S.A.
485 Fifth Avenue
New York, NY 10017-6104
Phone: (212) 697-3232

WORLD CONSTITUTION
AND PARLIAMENT
ASSOCIATION
1480 Hoyt Street, Suite 31
Lakewood, CO 80215
Phone: (303) 233-3548

NATIONAL PEACE
INSTITUTE FOUNDATION
110 Maryland Ave., N.E.
Washington, D.C. 20002
Phone: 1-800-237-3223

WORLD FEDERALISTS
OF CANADA
145 Spruce Street, Suite 207
Ottawa, Ontario K1R 6P1
Phone: (613) 232-0647

CAMPAIGN FOR WORLD
GOVERNMENT, INC.
552 Lincoln Avenue
Winnetka, IL 60093
Phone: (312) 446-7177 or
835-1377

Appendix 2
Highlights of the United Nations

The United Nations was created to prevent war by providing Governments with means for regular contact, cooperation, and collective action. Though international conflicts have continued, over the last 40 years Governments have been able to agree on common positions in a surprising number of matters. In the process, the essential foundations for a peaceful world have been strengthened. The United Nations system has become the world's main source of international law, codifying and creating more of it in four decades than in all previous history. In the area of human rights, its work has been pioneering. The protection of human rights is acknowledged now to be a legitimate concern of the international community: global standards have been set and binding agreements negotiated for the observance of a wide range of basic rights.

The United Nations has eased the passage to freedom of millions of people in former colonial territories, and focused international attention and support for ancient societies transforming themselves with modern science and technology. It has led a worldwide cooperative effort to deal with such urgent problems as population growth and environmental hazards, the effects of which transcend all national borders. For millions caught unprotected in the tumultuous processes of change—poor children, political refugees, victims of disaster—the Organization has brought the healing touch of attention and care. The chronology below is by no means a comprehensive listing; it merely indicates the vast scope of United Nations activities over the last four decades.

1945: On June 26 the Charter of the United Nations is signed in San Francisco. The Second World War has ended in Europe but continues in Asia; its end there coincides with the terrible dawn of the nuclear age. ● The U.N., created on October 24, is at the center of a system of specialized agencies, some newly founded, others created decades earlier.

1946: In January, the *General Assembly* meets for the first time, in London, and elects the members of the *Security Council,* the *Economic and Social Council,* and the *International Court of Justice.* ● The first resolution the Assembly adopts is on disarmament, on the peaceful use of nuclear energy. Over the next four decades, as the arms race spirals upward, the organization keeps the problem high on the international agenda. • Other major problems considered by the first Assembly: decolonization, racial discrimination in South Africa, and the growing violence between Arabs and Jews in Palestine. • In October the Assembly meets in New York, picked as headquarters for the organization. It establishes the *United Nations Children's Fund.* • The *Trusteeship Council* is set up.

1947: The Assembly adopts a plan that would, at the end of the British Mandate in Palestine in 1948, partition it into an Arab State and a Jewish State with Jerusalem under U.N. administration. The organization's involvement in the region continues unabated over the next four decades as it seeks peace with equity for all parties involved.

1948: The *Universal Declaration of Human Rights* is adopted without opposition in the Assembly, marking the first time in history that such a document is endorsed by the international community. • The cold war is at its height and the Secretary-General reports that the U.N. is virtually the only place where East and West have regular contact. • U.N. military observers are sent to the Middle East and South Asia. • International statistical services are resumed after an interruption of almost a decade as the U.N. Secretariat begins to collect, analyze, and publish data from around the world.

1949: Consultations initiated at the U.N. lead to a resolution of the crisis over Western access to the divided city of Berlin. • The Assembly creates an agency to look after the welfare of the hundreds of thousands of Palestinian refugees in the Middle East. • The U.N. and the specialized agencies begin the *Expanded Program of Technical Assistance* to help economic and social development in poorer countries. • Experts from more than 50 countries attend the *U.N. Scientific Conference on Conservation and Utilization of Resources.*

1950: The Security Council calls on member states to help the southern part of Korea repel invasion from the north. (The Soviet Union is absent from the Council then, in protest against the exclusion of the People's Republic of China from the U.N.) • At the initiative of the U.N., the *World Census Program* gets under way, aiming at a global head-count every decade: the first such assessment in history. • The *U.N. Cartographic Office* is set up and coordinates with governments involved in producing a map of the world on the millionth scale. • The Economic and Social Council (ECOSOC) adopts the *Standard International Trade Classification,* the basis on which all statistics on world trade are now gathered.

1951: The Office of *U.N. High Commissioner for Refugees,* established by the General Assembly, takes over from the *International Refugee Organization.* The conference convened by the Assembly adopts the *Convention on Refugees,* spelling out their rights and international standards for their treatment. ● ECOSOC Regional Commission for Asia initiates studies of the Mekong River that lead to one of the largest river basin development projects attempted internationally.

1952: The General Assembly broadens its consideration of racial discrimination in South Africa to take up the entire question of *apartheid,* overriding South African objections that it is a matter entirely within its domestic jurisdiction. Over the next four decades, the organization will be at the forefront of international efforts to fight a system of racism that the Assembly terms a "crime against humanity." ● The U.N. produces the first in a series of reports on the *World Social Situation.*

1953: Armistice in Korea results from initiatives made at the U.N. ● The *U.N. Opium Conference* in New York adopts an international protocol to control the production, trade, and use of the drug.

1954: The Secretary-General initiates quiet—and ultimately successful—negotiations for the release of American airmen held as prisoners of war in China. ● The *World Population Conference* convened by ECOSOC brings over 450 experts to Rome. They adopt no resolutions, but it is evident that current knowledge of population trends is insufficient for decisions on economic and social policy. ● First signs of a thaw in the cold war appear as the ECOSOC Regional Commission for Europe takes up trade relations between different economic systems. ● The U.N. High Commissioner for Refugees wins the first of two Nobel Peace Prizes; the second is awarded in 1981.

1955: The first *U.N. Congress on Prevention of Crime and Treatment of Offenders* sets minimum standards for the treatment of prisoners and for the training of personnel for correctional institutions. ● The first international conference on the *Peaceful Uses of Atomic Energy* convenes in Geneva and initiates a broad range of cooperation in the field.

1956: War in the Middle East over the Suez Canal is ended with the deployment of a U.N. peacekeeping force in the Sinai. ● A U.N.-supervised plebiscite in British Togoland leads to the merging of that Territory with the Gold Coast to form the new State of Ghana.

1957: In the wake of Sputnik, the General Assembly takes up the peaceful uses of outer space. In the following years, it elaborates a new body of law to cover the exploration and use of outer space, including the Moon and other celestial bodies. • The *International Atomic Energy Agency,* created by the General Assembly, begins work with headquarters in Vienna.

1958: The *U.N. Observer Group* helps defuse a Lebanon crisis. • The *Inter-Governmental Maritime Consultative Organization* begins work as a U.N. specialized agency, setting safe standards for shipping. • The first *U.N. Conference on the Law of the Sea* adopts four landmark Conventions. • French Togoland becomes indcpcndent after a U.N.-supervised plebiscite.

1959: The General Assembly adopts the *Declaration of the Rights of the Child.* • A *Special Fund* established by the General Assembly works in tandem with the *Expanded Program of Technical Assistance* to help developing countries explore areas into which private and public capital can be attracted. • A U.N.-supervised plebiscite in the British Cameroons results in a part of the Territory's being incorporated into Nigeria and another into the Cameroons.

1960: With the entry into the U.N. of 17 newly independent Territories, 16 of them African, the General Assembly assumes a much more active role in the process of decolonization. It adopts the *Declaration on the Granting of Independence to Colonial Countries and Peoples,* saying colonialism is a denial of basic human rights and calling for its swift end. • At the request of the newly independent State of Congo, the largest ever U.N. peacekeeping force takes the ficld in an effort to save that mineral-rich country from destabilization and preserve its tcrritorial integrity.

1961: Acknowledging that economic and social development in the poorer countries is basic to the achievement of international peace and security, the General Assembly declares the 1960's the *U.N. Development Decade.* U.N. capacity to deal with development problems is vastly increased during the decade.

1962: The Secretary-General plays a key role in resolving U.S.-Soviet confrontation over the issue of nuclear missiles in Cuba. • The U.N. takes over administration of Dutch West New Guinea before transferring power to Indonesia. • The *U.N. Observer Mission* aids peace efforts in Yemen.

1963: The U.N. and the Food and Agriculture Organization (FAO) set up the *World Food Program* to provide food and other commodity aid to needy countries, drawing on surpluses in donor countries. • The Security Council calls for voluntary arms embargo against South Africa.

1964: *U.N. Conference on Trade and Development* declares trade a "primary instrument of development," and calls for a permanent secretariat to focus on the web of problems involved. A

U.N. peacekeeping force is sent to Cyprus to keep communal peace. It stays over the following years as talks under U.N. auspices seek a peaceful solution.

1965: The *U.N. Observer Mission* helps disengagement of forces after war between India and Pakistan. ● Technical assistance activities get a big boost with the merger of the *Expanded Program* (1949) and the *Special Fund* (1959) to form the *U.N. Development Program* as the major channel of funding for the specialized agencies in the U.N. system. UNDP assumes an important coordinating role and extends a network of "resident representatives" to help aid delivery around the world. ● UNICEF is awarded the Nobel Peace Prize.

1966: Two major covenants on human rights are adopted, one covering *Civil and Political Rights* and the other *Economic, Social, and Cultural Rights.* The former has an "Optional Protocol" allowing individual complaints to be considered by the international *Human Rights Committee.* Together, the two binding instruments cover most of the rights included in the 1948 *Universal Declaration of Human Rights.* ● The Security Council, for the first time in U.N. history, imposes mandatory sanctions against Southern Rhodesia, where a racist white minority government unilaterally declared independence from Britain in 1965. ● The Assembly ends South Africa's mandate over the Territory of South West Africa, saying it has failed to fulfill its obligations.

1967: After war erupts again in the Middle East, the Security Council adopts Resolution 242, which calls for withdrawal of forces from occupied territories and recognizes the right of all States in the area to security. It becomes a widely accepted basis for a settlement of the Middle East problem. ● The General Assembly, meeting in special session, sets up a U.N. Council to administer South West Africa.

1968: On the 20th anniversary of the Universal Declaration, the *International Conference on Human Rights* is convened by the General Assembly in Teheran. The first worldwide governmental meeting on the whole range of human rights, it reaffirms the Declaration, and chalks out further priorities for U.N. action.

1969: *The Convention on Elimination of All Forms of Racial Discrimination,* adopted by the General Assembly in 1965, comes into force. Parties to the Convention condemn racial discrimination and *apartheid* and undertake to adopt policies for their elimination without delay.

1970: The *International Development Strategy* is adopted for the *Second Development Decade* declared by the General Assembly. Targets are set for different groups of countries and for increases in aid and industrial and agricultural production. • The General Assembly adopts the first internationally agreed set of principles on the vast area of seabed and ocean floor beyond national jurisdiction. The first principle declares the area to be the "common heritage" of humanity.

1971: The International Court of Justice, in an advisory opinion requested by the Security Council, declares the continued presence of South Africa in Namibia "illegal." • The Assembly restores "lawful rights" of the People's Republic of China in the U.N. • Bahrain becomes independent after the U.N. helps resolve an Iran-United Kingdom dispute on the status of territory. • Massive U.N. relief effort aids victims of conflict in East Pakistan (later Bangladesh).

1972: The U.N. *Environment Conference* meets in Stockholm and adopts a historic declaration on the need for new principles to govern human activities in order to safeguard the natural world. The Assembly sets up the *U.N. Environment Program* to catalyze action in that regard. • The *U.N. Disaster Relief Organization,* created by the General Assembly to keep tabs on and coordinate international aid in emergencies, becomes operational.

1973: Another war in the Middle East ends with new U.N. peacekeeping forces in the Sinai and the Golan Heights. • The Assembly bases *U.N. University* in Tokyo to coordinate and marshal efforts by the world's intellectual communities to deal with global problems.

1974: After a breakdown of the world monetary system of fixed currency exchange values, amidst energy and food crises, the Assembly calls for a *New International Economic Order* as a stable basis for interdependent world economy. • World conferences on population and food assess the current situation and underline need for a global change. • Inter-communal talks in Cyprus are convoked by the Secretary-General.

1975: *World Conference of the International Women's Year* convenes in Mexico City and adopts the *Declaration on Equality of Women and Their Contribution to Development and Peace.* A Plan of Action for the next ten years provides for world conferences to review progress at the mid-point and end of the *U.N. Decade for Women.*

1976: To deal with perennial problems of low and erratic prices of raw materials in world trade (on which most developing countries depend), the *U.N. Conference on Trade and Development* adopts the *Integrated Program* involving a new fund to finance buffer stocks and a range of individual commodity agreements. ● A conference on human habitat plans action.

1977: The Security Council makes the arms embargo against South Africa mandatory. ● The billion-dollar *International Fund for Agricultural Development,* a new U.N. specialized agency, begins to finance food production in developing countries.

1978: The General Assembly convenes in special session, for the first time on the topic of disarmament, and succeeds in drawing up a framework for future action and a set of priorities. ● The Security Council adopts a plan put forward by five Western countries for the independence of Namibia. ● A U.N. peace-keeping force is sent to Lebanon.

1979: The General Assembly adopts the *Convention on the Elimination of Discrimination Against Women,* covering political, economic, social, cultural, and civil rights.

1980: As the result of an international campaign coordinated by the *World Health Organization,* smallpox is totally eradicated from the world. The cost of the program to WHO is about what the world spends on arms in three hours.

1981: The General Assembly adopts *Declaration on Elimination of All Forms of Intolerance and Discrimination Based on Religion or Belief.* ● The *Conference on New and Renewable Sources of Energy* maps action.

1982: After nine years of complex and painstaking work, the Conference convened by the Assembly adopts what could be the most significant legal instrument of the century, the wide-ranging *Convention on the Law of the Sea.* ● Secretary-General Pérez de Cuéllar's first annual report to the Assembly warns of a trend toward world anarchy and urges rededication to Charter principles on the use of the U.N. as an instrument for peace and rational change.

1983: The Secretary-General visits southern Africa to consult on how the Security Council plan for independence of Namibia can be implemented. Virtually all outstanding issues are resolved, but South Africa's insistence on the withdrawal of Cuban troops from neighboring Angola before implementation of the plan makes its initiation impossible.

1984: After seven years of work in the *Commission on Human Rights,* the General Assembly adopts the *Convention Against Torture,* hailed as a major step toward creating a more humane world. ● The Assembly also adopts the Declaration on the critical economic situation and famine in Africa.

1985: The *Office for Emergency Operations,* created by the Secretary-General, spearheads a massive famine relief effort in Africa.

1986: The U.N. mobilizes a massive international aid program for drought-stricken African countries. ● In the aftermath of the Chernobyl accident, the *International Atomic Energy Agency* of the U.N. adopts two international conventions on early notification of atomic accidents and emergency mutual assistance. ● The Secretary-General of the U.N. successfully mediates the problem between New Zealand and France about the sinking of a Greenpeace boat.

1987: The *U.N. Environment Program* obtains international agreement and signature of a world convention on the protection of the ozonosphere. ● The U.N. convenes the first world conference on drug abuse and control of illicit traffic of drugs.

1988: The U.N. helps to bring about the withdrawal of Soviet troops from Afghanistan and to halt the fighting between Iran and Iraq U.N. peacekeeping forces monitor the situation. They are awarded the Nobel Peace Prize. ● The U.N. *Convention Against Illicit Traffic in Narcotic Drugs* is adopted in December.

1989: The U.N. establishes a special trust fund to enable even poor nations to bring disputes before the World Court. ● In January, 149 States unanimously call for the elimination of all chemical weapons. ● Plans are made for a conference in 1990 to deal with the problems of converting from military to civilian production. ● Steps are taken by the Secretary-General to ensure that Namibia will finally receive its independence in 1990. ● The General Assembly declares 1990-2000 the Decade of International Law.

1990: The Security Council, in an unprecedented and unanimous enforcement of the rule of law, imposed an escalating series of economic sanctions against Iraq for its August invasion of Kuwait. ● The U.N., led by its Secretary-General, after years of effort helped to halt the fighting in Nicaragua, to bring independence to Namibia and to move South Africa away from its inhumane support of apartheid. ● The *World Summit For Children,* organized by the U.N., brought over 70 world leaders together in October in an effort to save the lives of millions of children who now perish needlessly each year. ● The *International Law Commission* and the *U.N. Legal Committee* resumed consideration of an International Criminal Court to deal with drug trafficking and other international crimes.

Taken from *For a Better World* published by the United Nations, United Nations Plaza, New York, NY 10017

Appendix 3
World Government *IS* the First Step
by Emery Reves

The Anatomy of Peace by Emery Reves was presented in 1945 as a condensed book in *The Reader's Digest*. It was considered so important by the editors that they took two issues to review the book. Dr. Albert Einstein, Supreme Court Justice Owen J. Roberts, many Catholic, Jewish, and Protestant leaders, and representatives of business, labor, and veterans' organizations endorsed his plan to create world peace through world law. The *Reader's Digest* editors asked Emery Reves to comment on arguments that had been raised in the nationwide discussion of his ideas. The following appeared in *The Reader's Digest* issue of February, 1946.

Even those who, swayed by the logic of history or the eloquence of current events, see the importance of world government are likely to nod their heads and say, "Of course world government is the goal. But we can't get it immediately. We must proceed step by step."

Such a view overlooks the dire urgency of the problem created by the introduction of atomic fission into warfare. There is now no such thing as the first step toward world government. World government *is* the first step—the step that must be taken before there is any chance of meeting our other problems, economic and social. These problems will continue to exist, but the establishment of law rather than treaties among nations is essential if there is to be some framework within which these problems can be attacked. . . .

There is only one method that can create security against destruction by the atomic bomb. This is the same method that gives the states of New York and

California (nonproducers of the atomic bomb) security against being erased from the earth by the states of Tennessee and Washington (producers of the atomic bomb). It is the security given by a common sovereign order of law. Any other "security" is but an illusion.

No atomic bomb, no weapon that the genius of man can conceive, is dangerous in itself. Weapons become dangerous only when they are in the hands of sovereign states other than one's own. It follows that the ultimate source of danger is not atomic energy but the sovereign nation-state.

Five thousand years of history demonstrate that wars have ensued whenever social groups of equal sovereignty have come into contact. Peace between human beings has been possible only when their relations are regulated by law—a single system of law.

In our day and generation, the social groups in contact and in a state of permanent friction are the nation-states. So the problem is clearly defined: How can we stop wars between the nation-states?

The general belief is that we must have "some sort of international organization" to control wars. For centuries we have tried all sorts of international organizations, and we still insist that a workable world order be built upon a Bill of Rights without a Bill of Duties. The San Francisco Charter, far from explaining the cause of the world catastrophe and indicating the road to real freedom, again lures mankind toward the mirage of peace between sovereign states through treaties.

Peace by Law—Not by the U.N.

In a society without any system of law, no individual would ever trust a judge, a jury or a court, even if composed of the most eminent and selfless of his fellows. Members of a society are prepared to submit to one thing alone. To law. Such law is nonexistent among nations. It never did exist in international relations. It has been excluded from the League and from the United Nations Organization.

To base "peace" on unanimous decisions of a certain number of sovereign national governments—at present, on the unanimous decisions of the five greatest military powers—means indulging in a daydream. History proves beyond doubt that any real danger to world peace always emanates from one of the major military powers. It is clear that a major power will not cast its vote in any international council against its own interests. Consequently, in no major crisis will unanimous vote in the Security Council be obtainable. . . .

The fundamental problem of regulating the relations between great powers without the permanent danger of major wars cannot be solved so long as absolute sovereign power continues to reside in the nation-states. Unless their sovereign institutions are integrated into higher institutions, expressing directly the sovereignty of all peoples, conflicts between national units are inevitable.

In all current plans for a world organization all power, all decision, all action, all source of law, continues to rest with national governments. An organization of such sovereign nations, whether on an equal or unequal footing, could never prevent another war.

What matters it if the American Secretary of State, the Soviet Foreign Commissar and His Majesty's Foreign Secretary meet around a table as members of the United Nations Security Council or outside that organization in a Conference of Foreign Ministers? In either case they are but the sworn representatives of three sovereign nation-states; in either case the final decisions rest with Washington, Moscow and London. These representatives can only arrive at agreements or treaties and are without power to create law applicable to the individuals of their respective nation-states.

The present world crisis is not a new sort of crisis. And its solution is the same as has been applied many times in the past when conflicting and warring social units were integrated into a higher legal order. In the United States today, we have municipal governments to regulate the relations of men in towns and cities; we have state governments to regulate relations within states; and we have federal government to regulate relations within the federal union. Because of these three levels of governmental institutions, peace exists within towns and city communities, between them within the states, and between the states within the Union. . . .

In the light of past experience, this problem can be solved only by setting up a system of government on a *fourth* level—by instituting democratically controlled legislative, executive and judiciary bodies to regulate relations between people belonging to different nation-states.

Regulation in some form will come . . . because the highly integrated and unified industrial world . . . cannot develop within the present political nation-state framework created by the agricultural 18th century. This very same change we are approaching has been, in the overwhelming majority of cases, an extremely painful and bloody operation. It has usually been forced upon man by conquest. In only a few cases was it reached by persuasion, consent, union. . . .

Consider the Goal—Not the Difficulties

It is quite natural that the human mind should recoil from a concept so new and untested as the idea of world federal government. We think in terms of difficulties rather than in terms of our goal, and in consequence we permit ourselves to be lured into a series of bootless arguments over details. This prevents full consideration of the main point and blinds us to the fact that the details must be worked out only after there is agreement and consent among the peoples on the central aim.

Population figures are held up, like scarecrows, to frighten us away from our objective. How can we allow the Chinese or the Indians to outnumber us in a world legislative assembly?

The fact is that no Chinese or Indian has ever asked for representation based on population figures alone. In any universal government organization, representation will have to be determined by actual responsibility and according to effective power, industrial potential, degree of education. Various proved methods exist to work out this purely technical question.

But—people want to know—how can we think of giving foreigners the right to determine whether our boys should be sent overseas to fight?

This question completely misses the point. Within one generation our boys have actually been sent to fight two wars which were the exclusive decisions of Germany and Japan. It cannot be said that the United States or the British Commonwealth was "free to decide" whether its sons should go to war. The truth is that nations are today helpless marionettes, acting only as they are compelled to act by the actions of "foreign" countries. Our task is precisely to organize the world under law so that the peaceful existence of citizens will be protected. A police force, of course, is automatic and implicit. For only enforcement can give standing to any kind of law. But to establish an international police force without having previously established a world legislative assembly makes no sense.

Would a world government not destroy the nations?

On the contrary. It is the nation-state structure that is actually destroying nations today. A legal order alone can eliminate international wars and make secure the continued existence of nations and national cultures. A universal legal order, far from endangering in any way national and cultural differences, is today the *first* condition for the maintenance and continuous thriving of such differences. Without union, either the Scots would have exterminated the English or the English would have exterminated the Scots, just as the Romans destroyed Carthage and the Huns destroyed Rome. Within the United Kingdom the Scots are more Scottish in their traditions and character and the English more English in theirs than they ever were before that union.

Paradox it may seem, but it is only within a world-wide legal order that urges like patriotism or isolationism can be satisfied. There is nothing wrong with the desire for isolation. But there is something profoundly wrong with what today is called "isolationist policy." Where can an individual live an isolated life of his own? Certainly not in the physical isolation of a tropical jungle. There he has to be on guard day and night to preserve his life against beasts ready to prey on him. A man can live an isolated life in a civilized city where his security is guaranteed, where laws, courts and police watch over his physical existence and individual rights. Certainly no nation can safely live its own isolated life in the jungle of the present world.

Other skeptics raise the question: "What is the sense of stopping international wars by establishing an international government if we still will probably have to face revolutions and civil wars?"

This is like refusing surgery to someone suffering acute appendicitis because sometime after the operation he may catch pneumonia.

We must always keep in mind that there is no panacea for all problems of life and society. We can only cure specific diseases with specific remedies. The specific disease of our age is the acute friction between sovereign nation-states which manifests itself in the painful symptom of international war. That specific disease can be cured. And it must be cured, irrespective of future troubles human society may develop.

The most trying of all objections, of course, is the assertion made by so many "public figures": "The people are not yet ready for world federation."

One can only wonder how they know. Have they themselves ever advocated world federation? Do they themselves believe in it? Have they ever tried to explain to the people what makes war and what is the mechanism of peace in human society? And, after having understood the problem, have the people rejected the solution and decided they did not want peace by law and government but preferred war by national sovereignty? Until this happens, no one has the right to pretend he knows what the people are ready for. . . .

Hundreds of millions of civilized human beings—good-humored, honest, industrious, who could peacefully collaborate and enjoy life within one sovereignty—are being hoodwinked and bullied into senseless war. No amount of negotiating, of "good will" or wishful thinking will change this course. Only a clear realization by the people as to what is driving them into that conflict can bring about its eradication and cure. . . .

What Can We Do Now?

How can we go about trying to achieve peace by law?

Nothing is more futile than to work out detailed plans for a constitutional document of a world government. Such a procedure would only hinder progress. If at the very inception of democracy a specific draft of a democratic constitution had been identified with democracy itself, and put forward for general approval and acceptance, we should never have had a democratic state anywhere in the world.

History does not work that way.

The founders of democracy were much wiser. They first formulated a small number of fundamental principles. These principles succeeded in arousing the vision and inflaming the enthusiasm of the peoples who, on the basis of these ideas, empowered their representatives to translate them into reality and create the machinery necessary for a permanent legal order.

The constitutions, the fundamental laws of the new democratic order, were debated *after*, not before, the acceptance of the elementary principles and the mandate given by the people to their representatives. So today we see democracy expressed in systems of great variety in detail, but nonetheless deriving from identical principles.

Democracy in the United States is different from British democracy. French democracy is different from the Dutch, and Swiss democracy has institutions differing greatly from Swedish democracy. In spite of their differences in detail, they are all workable forms of democracy, expressing the same fundamental social conception, the sovereignty of the people. . . .

Regarding the creation of universal democratic legal order, we have not yet reached the state of conception. We have not yet formulated the principles. Five stages are clearly visible on the road from ideal to realization:

1. Conception of the idea, the proclamation of principles.

2. The doctrine must be spread in the same way Christianity, democracy and other successful doctrines were diffused.

3. Elect representatives, delegating to them the power to put into practice the new principles.

4. It is for these elected delegates to debate programs, to fight out details and to arrive at solutions for organizing world government to prevent wars between the nation-states.

5. Once this first constitutional step is taken, a great number of solutions will be more or less workable.

This is how history works. This is the way democratic constitutions were established in the 18th century.

This should in no way be discouraging. In this modern world of ours, with mass circulation newspapers, motion pictures and radio capable of reaching the entire civilized population of the earth, a decade is ample time for a movement to bring to triumph the principles of peace and universal law.

The movement needed to create world government must come from many lands. The essential thing is to find people of more than one country willing and eager to undertake it. There is evidence that such people can be found. In an historic speech made in the House of Commons on November 23, 1945, Foreign Secretary

Bevin, expressing his worry about "whether again the people would be disappointed" by what has been accomplished in San Francisco, declared:

> I feel we are driven relentlessly along this road: we need a new study for the purpose of creating a world assembly elected directly from the people of the world, as a whole, to whom the governments that formed the United Nations are responsible and who, in fact, make the world law which they, the people, will then accept and be morally bound and willing to carry out. I am willing to sit with anybody, of any party, of any nation, to try to devise a franchise or a constitution for a world assembly, with a limited objective—the objective of peace.

There is no short cut. The *people* must understand the problem; *they* must decide whether they want peace; *they* must impose their will on their representatives. The present governments of the nation-states will never undertake the required institutional changes. We must not forget that we are living in a democracy, that we have to go through the democratic process of debate and persuasion to arrive at changes in our society. Once the electors understand the problem and make their stand, the change in the stand of their representatives will be automatic.

Undoubtedly, if the inhabitants of another planet suddenly descended upon the earth and threatened to conquer us, all the nations of our small world would immediately get together. We would forget all our ridiculous international quarrels and willingly place ourselves under one rule of law for sheer survival. Are we certain that the apocalypse of an atomic world war is not an equal threat to our civilization and to mankind? . . .

Every citizen who believes in law and government in international relations must persuade ten other citizens of the same belief, and urge each to persuade,

179

on his behalf, ten more—at once. The nuclear physicists have explained that atomic energy is released by what is called a chain reaction. One atom is split. The released particles split other atoms, and so on. The force of ideas explodes in the form of just such a chain reaction.

We must persuade as many newspapers as possible to adopt the federal outlook as their editorial policy. This principle must also be constantly disseminated on the radio and in films. We must get this problem discussed in groups, meetings and on platforms. Universalism and the imperative need for universal law must resound in all houses of God. The universal outlook of political and social matters must be taught in all schools. We should elect nobody to public office who has not pledged . . . in advance to work wholeheartedly for preventing the next war by the establishment of peace through law and government.

An irresistible popular demand must be made articulate in every country as soon as possible. And when in two or more countries the people have clearly expressed their will, the process of federation must start. Naturally the ideal solution would be if all the people of the world were persuaded simultaneously. But such a course is unlikely. The process must start at the earliest possible moment, even with a minimum of two countries, because no argument can compare with the overwhelming persuasive power of events. There can be no question that, once the process of international integration starts, its attraction will be so great that more and more nations will join until finally, by the force of events, we shall arrive at a federal world government. . . .

We cannot achieve peace if all of a sudden we become satisfied with what is complacently accepted as a "first step." Every time our foreign ministers or the heads of our governments meet and decide not to decide, hurry to postpone, and commit themselves to no commitments, the official heralds proclaim jubilantly to the universe: "This is a hopeful beginning; this is a first step in the right direction." We shall never have peace if we do not have the courage to understand what it is, if we do not want to pay the price it costs.

Therefore the problem is: How willing are we to fight for the dissemination in schools, churches, meetings, the press, the movies and on the radio of a new faith, a new political outlook? This faith cannot take practical shape until enough people understand it, believe in it, want it.

Appendix 4
Circulate the Proclamation!

> *We seek to strengthen the United Nations, to help solve its financial problems, to make it a more effective instrument for peace, to develop it into a genuine world security system ... capable of resolving disputes on the basis of law, of insuring the security of the large and the small, and of creating conditions under which arms can finally be abolished. .... This will require a new effort to achieve world law.*
>
> **John F. Kennedy**
> Former U.S. President
>
> *Spaceship Earth tumbles through space with no one at the helm and with its life support system running down. We're the passengers. But we're also the crew. We're the ones who can save the ship! And if we are to save this planet, its problems will have to be tackled at the planetary level. Global problems respect no national borders: pollution knows no nationality.*
>
> **"It's Your Earth"**
> World Federalist Association

For the Future of Humanity!

If you believe that the human species should not become extinct upon this planet, and you want the five billion people on earth to live in lasting harmony with each other and the environment, please add your name.

You can make a difference by copying this proclamation and circulating it as widely as possible. When sheets are full, mail them to your political leaders and to Mr. Javier Pérez de Cuéllar, Secretary-General, United Nations, New York, NY 10017-0000. You will be showing them how much the people of this world want to get rid of world anarchy and enjoy lasting peace.

PROCLAMATION!
My Ultimate Human Right

I have the right to live with dignity in a healthy environment free from the threat of war.

Goal: Millions of signatures as rapidly as possible.

Name	Country

Mail to your President, U.S. Senator or Representative, and Secretary-General, United Nations, N.Y., NY 10017-0000.

Acknowledgments

We wish to acknowledge the unacknowledged contributions to this book that have been made by so many people. In a book written for a broad audience, we felt it would be inappropriate to footnote every phrase or idea as in scholarly presentations. Our deep thanks and appreciation go out to all who have contributed to the mainstream of ideas that helps us understand what each of us must do to give our children a life on this planet.

Professor Robert H. Manley of Seton Hall University; Robert Muller, with 38 years of service in the U.N.; and Rear Admiral Gene R. LaRocque, U.S. Navy (Ret.), director, Center for Defense Information kindly consented to read the manuscript for accuracy. We especially appreciate the suggestions of Walter Hoffman, executive director of the World Federalist Association. We have benefited by the inspiration and vision of *The Anatomy of Peace* by Emery Reves. Wendy Reves has graciously given permission to quote from her husband's work. Joy Huntley contributed many excellent editorial suggestions.

Eric Cox of the Campaign for U.N. Reform deserves recognition for having inspired the preparation of this book. He also helped by furnishing source material. Gertrude Ferencz has been a constant source of comfort, encouragement, and enlightenment. Martin Segal of Florida and Donald Ferencz also gave many thoughtful suggestions. Dick Trostler of Claremont, California offered helpful criticism.

Penny Keyes greatly assisted with the editing and proofreading. Ann Hauser generously contributed her artistic talents and brilliantly did the complicated typesetting. Karen Stephenson contributed to the cover design. Marci Figone assisted with editorial suggestions and transcribed the manuscript. Meg Studer (with revisions by Lynne Tuft) donated the original drawing used throughout the book that illustrates the spirit of planetary cooperation. Rik Burkhart suggested the title *PlanetHood*. Marjorie Tully did the final editing.

Appreciation is given to the following authors and publishers for quotations in this book: Harper and Row from *Union Now* by Clarence Streit and *The World Must Be Governed* by Vernon Nash; Richard Hudson of the Center for War/Peace Studies for material on the Binding Triad; the Campaign for U.N. Reform for "A 14-Point Program for Reforming the United Nations"; Tom Hudgens for permission to quote from *Let's Abolish War;* the American Movement for World Government for "Essentials of a World Federal Government"; The *New York Times* for the Robert D. McFadden article on Earth Day 1990; Little, Brown and Company for excerpts from *Miracle at Philadelphia* by Catherine Drinker Bowen and excerpts from *Peace or Anarchy* by Cord Meyer; Viking Penguin for quotations by Carl Van Doren from *The Great Rehearsal: The Story of Making and Ratifying the Constitution of the United States;* and *Reader's Digest* for Emery Reves' "World Government *IS* the First Step." To these and other sources, we offer our deepest appreciation.

We are particularly appreciative to those many thoughtful readers who have ordered *PlanetHood* by the hundreds and thousands to distribute widely, and to the many friends who have written from all parts of the world expressing encouragement and support.

Benjamin B. Ferencz
New Rochelle, New York

Ken Keyes, Jr.
Coos Bay, Oregon

Other Love Line Books

Handbook to Higher Consciousness
Ken Keyes, Jr., $6.95

Why are our lives filled with turmoil and worry? *Handbook to Higher Consciousness* presents practical methods that can help you create unconditional love and happiness in your life. Countless people have experienced a dramatic change in their lives from the time they began applying the effective techniques explained in the *Handbook*. There are over one million in print worldwide.

Handbook to Higher Consciousness: The Workbook
Ken and Penny Keyes, $7.95

Filled with three months of worksheets, this workbook is geared for the busy person. In 15 to 20 minutes a day, you can begin to apply the methods presented in *Handbook to Higher Consciousness* in your day-to-day interactions with yourself and others. Each day you are gently guided to uncover those roadblocks that are keeping you from experiencing the most enjoyable life possible. Based on years of practice by thousands of "living lovers," this workbook offers the daily practice you need to get results. It is a great way to get it working in your life!

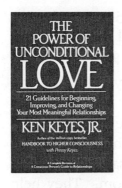

The Power of Unconditional Love: 21 Guidelines for Beginning, Improving, and Changing Your Most Meaningful Relationships

Ken Keyes, Jr., $8.95

You are shown how the enormous of power of unconditional love can enable you to create a wonderful trust and comfort with the diverse issues, different backgrounds, and changing wants and interests of your loved ones. It contains guidelines to help you prepare yourself for a relationship that can fulfill your heart's desire for love and intimacy. Additional guidelines help make your relationship richer and more delightful. Also offered are guidelines for how you can let go of a relationship with love and wisdom.

Gathering Power Through Insight and Love

Ken and Penny Keyes, $6.95

Here's how to do it! This outstanding book gives you detailed instructions on exactly how to develop the love inside you. Its goal is practical, how-to-do-it techniques you can use to handle upsetting situations in your life. It describes the 2-4-4 System for going from the separate-self to the unified-self: 2 Wisdom Principles, 4 Living Love Methods, and 4 Dynamic Processes. This book is based on the authors' years of leading workshops. These skills are essential for those who want the most rapid rate of personal growth using the Science of Happiness.

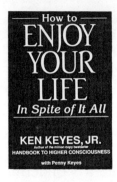

How to Enjoy Your Life in Spite of It All
Ken Keyes, Jr., $8.95

Learn to enjoy your life, no matter what others say or do! The Twelve Pathways explained in this book are a modern, practical condensation of thousands of years of accumulated wisdom. They help us remember when our egos blind us. Using these proven pathways will help you change your mental habits from separating, ineffective reactions to practical, loving ways for making your life work better. They promote deeper levels of insight and help increase your energy, inner peace, love, and perceptiveness in your moment-by-moment living. A must for people who are sincerely interested in their personal growth. 90,000 in print.

Your Life Is a Gift
Ken Keyes, Jr., $6.95

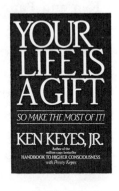

Presented in a lighthearted and delightful fashion, here is a wonderful introduction to ways you can create your own happiness. This charming book, geared toward those embarking on personal growth, shows how simple it is to experience life with joy and purpose by insightfully guiding your thoughts and actions. Every other page has an amusing and endearing drawing by Ann Hauser. Reading time is about one hour. This is a treasured gift book for everyone. 200,000 in print.

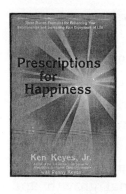

Prescriptions for Happiness
Ken Keyes, Jr., $5.95

Use these easy-to-remember secrets for happiness that work for both children and adults. Designed for busy people, this book can be absorbed in about an hour. These three simple prescriptions can work wonders in your life. They help you put more fun and aliveness into your interactions with people. They help you learn to ask for what you want with love in your heart. You can benefit from these three techniques that boost insight, love, and enjoyment in everyday situations. Some people, after reading this book, have bought out the bookstore to give copies to their friends. 159,000 in print.

Taming Your Mind
Ken Keyes, Jr., $7.95

This enjoyable classic (which has been in print for 40 years and is more relevant today than ever) shows you how to use your mind more effectively. Explains six "Tools for Thinking" that can enormously improve your success in making sound decisions, getting along with people, being more effective in business—and helping to build a better world. Written in an entertaining style with drawings by famous cartoonist Ted Key, it was adopted by two national book clubs. Over 125,000 copies in print.

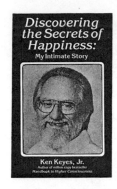

Discovering the Secrets of Happiness: My Intimate Story
Ken Keyes, Jr., $7.95

In this inspiring story, Ken shares his own journey of inner growth from being an unfulfilled man seeking happiness through money and sex to becoming a respected teacher of personal growth and world peace. Ken candidly describes his successes and failures as he recounts how he gave up a lucrative business to dedicate his life to serving others. It tells how he has successfully harnessed the power of "superlove" to create a deeply fulfilling marriage with Penny. He shows how you can enormously benefit from applying the secrets he discovered.

The Hundredth Monkey
Ken Keyes, Jr., Pocketbook, $2.50

There is no cure for nuclear war— ONLY PREVENTION! You are introduced to a new way of realizing your impact on the world around you— a quantum leap in consciousness. The people of our planet must use their grassroots energy to halt the suicide of the human race. You'll find here the facts about our nuclear predicament that some people don't want you to know. It gives details on our terrible killing power that could wipe out humanity. It can be read in a little over an hour. Internationally acclaimed, over one million copies have been distributed throughout the world. This dynamic little book has been translated into nine languages, including Russian.

PlanetHood

Benjamin B. Ferencz and Ken Keyes, Jr.

Trade edition, $7.95
Pocketbook edition, $2.50

This breakthrough book, which is the sequel to *The Hundredth Monkey*, explains what must be done to give ourselves and our families a future in this scientific age. It tells how we can replace the *law of force* with the *force of law*. It explains eight ways you can personally help the world settle disputes *legally*—instead of *lethally!* Discover this workable, practical way you can play your part in bringing prosperity and permanent peace to our planet.

Meeting the Challenge

You can empower yourself to make a difference. Since your future and the life of your family may depend on rapidly replacing the law of force with the force of law, we are making *PlanetHood* available for as low as 50¢ per copy postpaid! Please buy as many copies as you can and distribute them quickly.

To help you do this, the list price of the pocketbook size of *PlanetHood* is $2.50. For only $3 postpaid, we will mail a copy to any person in the world for whom you furnish the name and address. If you buy a case of 100, we will mail the case anywhere in the United States at a cost of only 70¢ per book (a total of $70 postpaid in the U.S.). If you buy 1,000 or more, they will cost only 50¢ per book (a total of $500 including shipping in the U.S.). Send orders to Ken Keyes College Bookroom, 790 Commercial Avenue, Coos Bay, OR 97420. For VISA or MasterCard orders call (503) 267-4112 or toll free 1-800-545-7810.

All these books are available in bookstores or see page 192 for order form.

TO ORDER BOOKS (See pages 186-191)

Qty.	Item	Price	Amount

Please include shipping and handling charges:
$1.50 first item, 50¢ for each additional item.

Subtotal	
Shipping	
TOTAL	

☐ **Yes!** Please put me on your mailing list and send me a free catalog listing workshops, books, posters, and audio and video tapes.

Ship to: (please print) _____

Address _____

City _____

State _____ Zip_____

Telephone No. ( ) _____

For ( ) VISA or ( ) MasterCard orders only:

Card # _____

Exp. Date _____ Signature: _____

Ken Keyes' books may be purchased through any bookstore. For mail order, send your check in U.S. funds or credit card information to Ken Keyes College Bookroom, Suite 14, 790 Commercial Avenue, Coos Bay, OR 97420. To order by phone with VISA or MasterCard call: 1-800-545-7810 or in Oregon (503) 267-4112, Monday through Friday, 9:00 a.m. to 4:30 p.m. Pacific time.

Index